CW01514219

Predators

OF SOUTHERN AFRICA
A FIELD GUIDE

HANS GROBLER

ANTHONY HALL-MARTIN

CLIVE WALKER

SOUTHERN
BOOK PUBLISHERS

Copyright © 1984, 1988 by Hans Grobler, Anthony Hall-Martin, Clive Walker

All rights reserved. No part of this production may be
reproduced, or transmitted, in any form or by any means
without prior written permission from the publisher.

ISBN 1 86812 276 X

First edition, first impression 1988
Second edition, first impression 1989 by

Southern Book Publishers (Pty) Ltd
PO Box 548, Bergvlei 2012
Johannesburg

Originally published by
Macmillan South Africa (Publishers) (Pty) Ltd

Cover design by Michael Barnett
Set in Century by Gammagraphic, Johannesburg
Printed and bound by National Book Printers, Cape

Contents

List of colour illustrations	7
Foreword	9
Preface	10
Acknowledgements	12
Introduction	13

Jackals, Foxes, Wild Dog   15

Side-striped jackal	16
Black-backed jackal	20
Cape fox	22
Bat-eared fox	24
African wild dog	26

Polecats, Weasels, Honey Badger, Otters   31

Striped polecat	32
White-naped weasel	34
Honey badger	36
Clawless otter	40
Spotted-necked otter	42

Civets, Genets, Mongooses, Suricate   43

African civet	44
Palm civet	46
Small-spotted genet	52
Rusty-spotted genet	54
White-tailed mongoose	56
Meller's mongoose	58
Water mongoose	64
Large grey mongoose	66
Cape grey mongoose	67
Slender mongoose	69
Dwarf mongoose	73
Banded mongoose	75
Yellow mongoose	77
Selous' mongoose	79
Suricate	80
Bushy-tailed mongoose	84

Hyaenas and Aardwolf   85

Spotted hyaena   86
Brown hyaena   89
Aardwolf   96

Cats   98

African wild cat   99
Black-footed cat   101
Serval   107
Caracal   109
Lion   111
Leopard   117
Cheetah   120

Photographs of Predators' Droppings in the Field   127
List of scientific names of animals mentioned in the text   131
Index   133

List of Colour Illustrations

Side-striped jackal	17
Black-backed jackal	17
Cape fox	18
Bat-eared fox	27
African wild dog	28
Striped polecat	37
White-naped weasel	37
Honey-badger	38
Clawless otter	38
Spotted-necked otter	47
African civet	48
Palm civet	49
Small-spotted genet	50
Rusty-spotted genet	50
White-tailed mongoose	59
Meller's mongoose	60
Water mongoose	60
Cape grey mongoose	61
Large grey mongoose	61
Dwarf mongoose	62
Banded mongoose	71
Yellow mongoose	72
Selous' mongoose	72
Suricate	81
Slender mongoose	82
Brown hyaenas, foraging	91
Brown hyaena	91
Spotted hyaena	92,93
Aardwolf pups	94
African wild cat	103
Black-footed cat	104
Serval	105
Caracal	106
Caracal kittens	115
Lioness	116
White lion cubs	116
Lion	121
Leopard	122
Cheetah	123
'King cheetah'	124

Foreword

The African fauna is richly endowed with carnivores, ranging from the tiny dwarf mongoose to the mighty lion, utilising food from the smallest insect to large prey animals like the buffalo and the giraffe.

Carnivores stir man's imagination. Is it because of man's own past as a hunter, or is it because the two animals that man has domesticated as house pets are both carnivores, or can it be attributed to the majesty and strength radiated by a lion?

Whatever the case may be, because of the emotion predators arouse in us, it is difficult to look at them objectively and, as the authors state in the introduction to this book, even nature lovers are sometimes strangely antagonistic towards predators.

Although it is not stated as such, one of this book's primary aims is to put our South African carnivores in their true perspective, to see them for what they really are.

Hans Grobler, Anthony Hall-Martin and Clive Walker are well known in wildlife circles. They all have the one important attribute to write a book of this nature: personal experience of the animals they are writing about.

This fact becomes evident as one reads through the text. Apart from a brief description of each animal, there are notes on the distribution, habitat, behaviour, habits and breeding of each of the 36 species of carnivores occurring in Southern Africa.

Drawings of the skull, coloured photographs, illustrations of the spoor and droppings, and distribution maps make this a valuable field guide to our predator community.

This book is more than a field guide, however, because it will be a valuable aid not only for identifying our carnivores, but also for depicting them for what they are: predators that live off the land, each one occupying a particular niche according to its size and prey preference.

Although the authors clearly state that the book is not written in defence of carnivores, it will certainly contribute towards seeing carnivores not only as killers but also as wildlife managers who maintain the ecological equilibrium of their respective communities.

PROFESSOR FRITZ ELOFF

Chairman of the National Parks Board of Trustees.

Preface

'Harmony with land is like
harmony with a friend; you
cannot cherish his right
hand and chop off his left
you cannot love game
and hate predators . . .'
ALDO LEOPOLD

Many lovers of nature and wildlife are strangely antagonistic towards predators. Perhaps this stems from the age-old conflict between farmers and herders and the flesheaters. The carnivores are seen as vermin, as a threat to poultry and livestock. Obviously, one cannot keep livestock and retain a spectrum of large predators on the same property. But this antagonism towards predators is often directed at innocent animals — perhaps because the role of carnivores in the animal community is so frequently misunderstood.

Steel-jawed traps and poison continue to be used indiscriminately against predators. In some areas campaigns are encouraged by the authorities in the name of rabies control and problem animal control. Bounties are still paid for the pelts of some species. Though some carnivores such as black-backed jackal and lynx are indeed a problem to smallstock in some areas, indiscriminate eradication of all carnivores is not the ecologically sound answer. Because large-scale eradication of predators, unlike sport hunting, is seldom selective, many individuals of sometimes locally rare or endangered species are killed. Not only do the predatory mammals die, but the raptors — the large flesh eating birds — are also affected. Some species have almost vanished over vast ranges where they were formerly abundant.

A mention of carnivores or predators usually brings to mind the large animals — lion, leopard or hyaena. Yet most of the Southern African carnivores are small animals, and 20 out of the 36 species weigh 5 kg or less. They range in size from the dwarf mongoose at about 0,35 kg to the African lion, which weighs up to 225 kg. Some are aquatic, like the otters; some are largely arboreal, like the genets and palm civet; some are nocturnal, others diurnal. The carnivores are adapted for catching and killing live prey, but each family has its peculiarities and each species its own ecological niche or function in nature. Some carnivores eat other carnivores, and some even kill and eat their own kind. Others eat a good deal of vegetable matter, but one must consider what represents the principal food of the species: because a jackal is seen eating a watermelon does not mean it could survive on them; because a bat-eared fox may eat a small antelope does not alter the fact that it feeds mainly on insects and small rodents.

Our knowledge of the small carnivores in particular is poor, and our understanding of the role that they play in farming areas is especially weak. Most of the studies that have been done on these animals were carried out in conservation areas. It is now necessary to look at carnivores as part of the wildlife system, which functions in parallel with man and his domestic stock.

We have not, however, written this book in defence of carnivores, but as a simple guide to assist in their identification. This knowledge will, we hope, stimulate an interest in our predators and foster an understanding of their diversity and complexity, and of the desirability of maintaining them as part of our living world.

Perhaps in time to come we will have a better understanding of the carnivores, some of which may be among the most endangered of our large mammals. Fortunately, most carnivores breed readily in captivity, but it will be a sad day for mankind when the last remaining lions are confined to zoos and artificial 'lion parks', or when the last African wild dogs have been driven from the plains forever.

Acknowledgements

We gratefully acknowledge the help we have received from many colleagues and friends. In particular Dr M.G.L. Mills for commenting on the manuscript and providing colour transparencies. Others who have contributed information or pictures, or provided assistance in other ways are: Anthony Bannister, Dr Frank Brand, Colin Britz, Willie de Beer, Anne van Dyk, Catherina Hall-Martin, William Massyn, Dr D. Mason, Garth Owen-Smith, Dr U. de V. Pienaar, Laurie Smith, Lorna Stanton, A. Seydack, Peter Steyn, Chris Stuart, Slang Viljoen, Zelda Wahl and Pat Wolff. We also thank the Director and Staff of the National Parks Board and in particular Mr P. van Wyk, Head of Research and Information. Our thanks to Eleanor-Mary Cadell of Macmillan whose patient editing and advice have been greatly appreciated.

Finally, our thanks to Merle Whyte for typing the manuscript and Helga Knoester for drawing the maps.

The scientific nomenclature used for the carnivores follows R.H.N. Smithers (1983), *The Mammals of the Southern African Subregion,* University of Pretoria, Pretoria. The drawings of palm civet and Meller's mongoose spoor are also based on Dr Smithers' work.

The colour photographs that are reproduced in this book were taken by the following:

Anthony Bannister: 106; Cape Department of Nature and Environmental Conservation: 38 (foot), 94; Willie de Beer: 91 (top), 104; Hans Grobler: 18 (top), 37 (top), 61 (top), 115; Anthony Hall-Martin: 17, 28, 62, 71, 92, 93, 116 (top), 121; F.W. Lane: 47; Gus Mills: 18 (foot), 122 (top); National Parks Board: 27, 38 (top), 50 (foot), 59, 81, 82, 103; U. de V. Pienaar: 60 (top); Dick Reucassel, F.R.P.S.: 48, 124; Alan Root: Survival Anglia: 49; Lorna Stanton: 72 (top); Peter Steyn: 72 (foot); Chris Stuart: 37 (foot), 50 (top), 60 (foot), 61 (foot); Zelda Wahl, Cape Department of Nature and Environmental Conservation: 91 (foot); Pat Wolff: 116 (foot), 122 (foot); Clive Walker: 123; Roger De la Harpe: 105.

Numbers refer to the pages on which illustrations occur.

Introduction

This book, like most field guides, is essentially a compilation of our own observations and records and information from the personal communications of colleagues and from published literature. Some of the 36 species of carnivores included are quite well documented, while others are almost unknown.

The book covers the area of Southern Africa, which is taken as a line drawn from the Cunene River in the west to the Zambezi River in the east, and between them the southern political boundaries of Angola and Zambia. The distribution maps are intended as a guide to the reader. They are based on the best available information, but do not include records of vagrant animals or introductions to small conservation areas. The scale of these maps is not such that small areas of absence can be shown. Nor have we tried to distinguish between areas of continuous and locally discontinuous distribution. Thus the areas for the hyaenas, which are extremely patchily distributed in farming land, are shown with the same hatching in the figures as that of an ubiquitous species like the polecat.

Because many of the carnivores are elusive and nocturnal, especially where they are hunted, illustrations of their spoor and droppings are included. Line drawings of the skulls are also included to assist in the identification of species from skeletal material. It will be seen from these drawings that the skulls differ in shape and size; also that, although all carnivores have well-developed canines, their cheek teeth (premolars and molars) vary in shape, size and number. Those of the aardwolf are reduced to a few stumps as there is no need for the animal to chew, the hyaenas have large bone-crushers, while the Meller's mongoose has flat ones suited to crushing termites and other insects.

In a book of this nature it is frequently necessary to generalise. This necessarily results in a 'loss' of information and in some cases may be quite misleading for a particular locality. Furthermore, there are many examples of carnivores adopting different behaviour according to prevailing circumstances in different areas.

There is still confusion over the common names of some predators: the 'draaijakkals' may be a Cape fox or a bat-eared fox depending on where you live; the black-footed cat and African wildcat are invariably confused. We have used the names that we feel are best suited to the different species and those that are most widely accepted.

JACKALS, FOXES, WILD DOG FAMILY CANIDAE

These dog-like carnivores with bushy tails and large, erect ears are light-footed and designed for running. They have long muzzles with an almost full complement of cheek teeth adapted for cutting meat, crushing insects or chewing, depending on the species. The jackals and foxes have five toes on the front feet and four on the hind, while the wild dog has only four on each. This family generally produces large litters, but numbers are presently kept in check by intense persecution from man. The family is represented by five species in the region: the side-striped jackal, black-backed jackal, Cape fox, bat-eared fox and African wild dog.

SIDE-STRIPED JACKAL
Canis adustus (Sundevall, 1846)

A: Witkwasjakkals

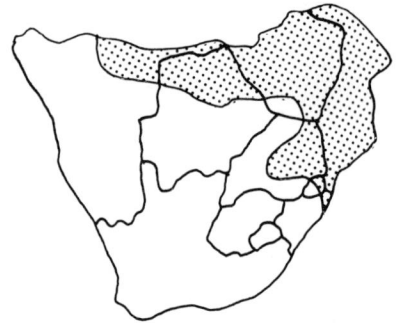

DESCRIPTION

A wolf-like jackal, grey in colour with a contrasting stripe on the flank and a characteristic white tip to the tail. The underparts and
throat are paler, sometimes tawny, while
the ears are smaller in relation to its body
than in other species of this family. It stands
about 40 cm at the shoulder and has a mass
of up to 12 kg. Head and body measurements are 65–80 cm; the tail is 30–40 cm
long.

DISTRIBUTION AND HABITAT

This is a species of the better watered
savanna regions, common in tall grassveld
and open woodland in the northern parts of
the region. Found in northern Botswana,
north-eastern SWA/Namibia, most of
Zimbabwe except the south-west, north-
eastern Transvaal, northern Natal and
Mozambique.

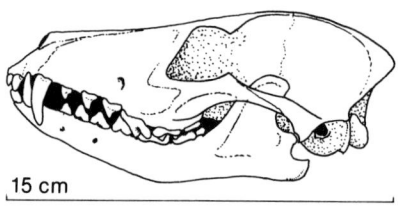

15 cm

FEEDING BEHAVIOUR

The diet is similar to that of the black-
backed jackal but this species does not
scavenge to the same extent. Feeds mainly
on insects, other invertebrates, small
rodents, various agricultural crops, such as
maize and groundnuts, and a variety of wild
fruit including *Diospyros* species, wild figs
and *Ziziphus mucronata* berries. Will also
eat birds when the opportunity arises. As
this animal does not appear to molest
poultry or livestock, but eats agricultural
pests, it is generally a useful animal to have
on farmland.

Actual Size

Opposite
Top: The side-striped jackal is predominantly grey in colour with a whitish throat, relatively
small ears and a characteristic stripe on the flank.

Below: The black-backed jackal has large ears, a black tail and silvery black saddle separated
from the red-brown flanks by a black stripe.

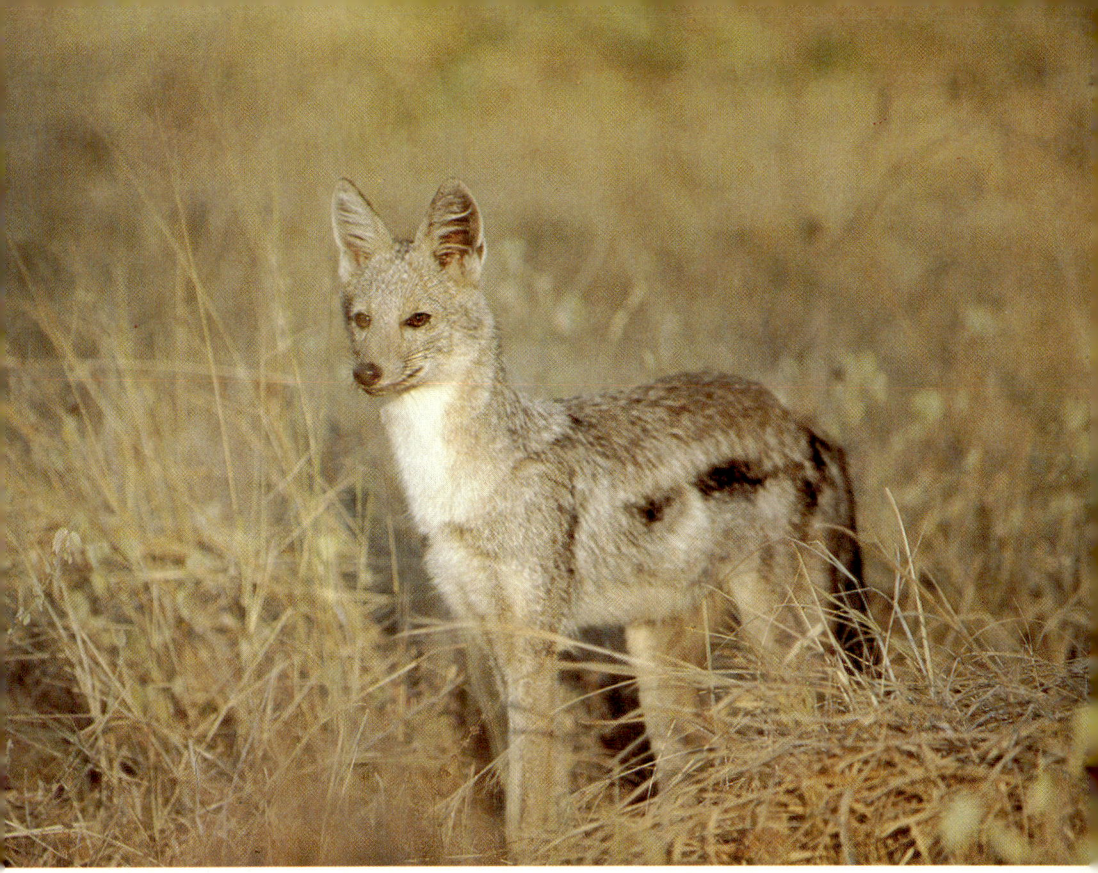

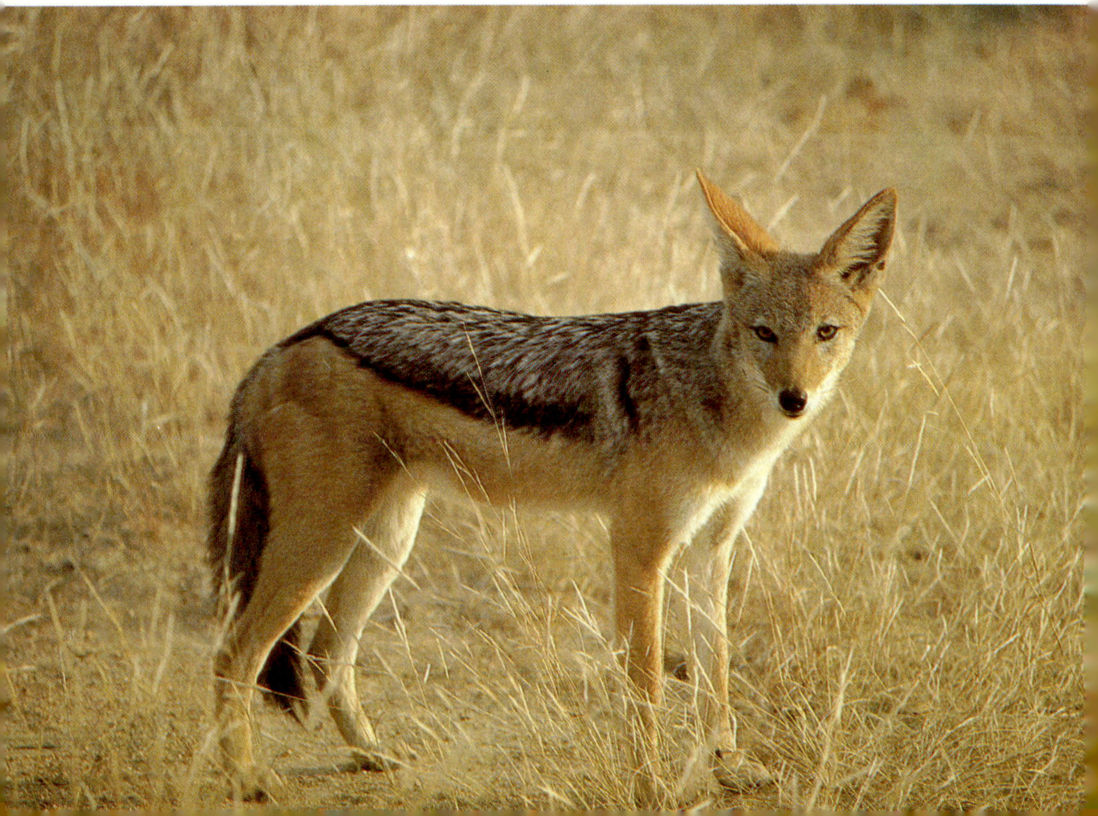

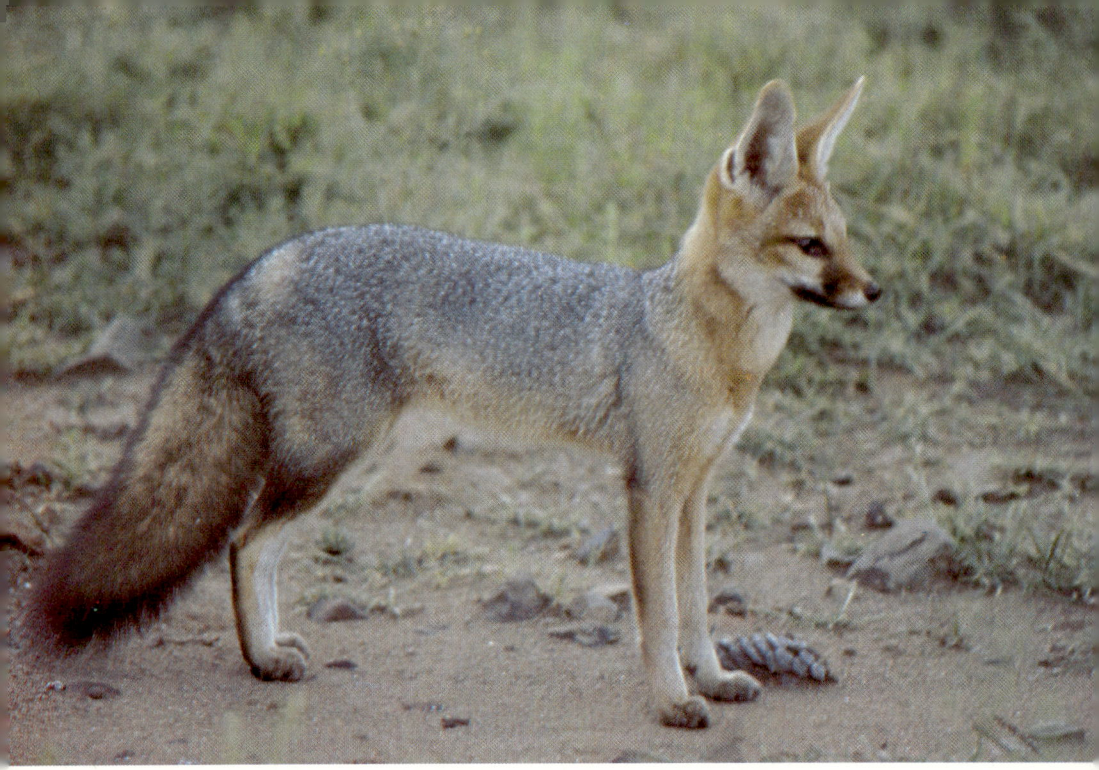

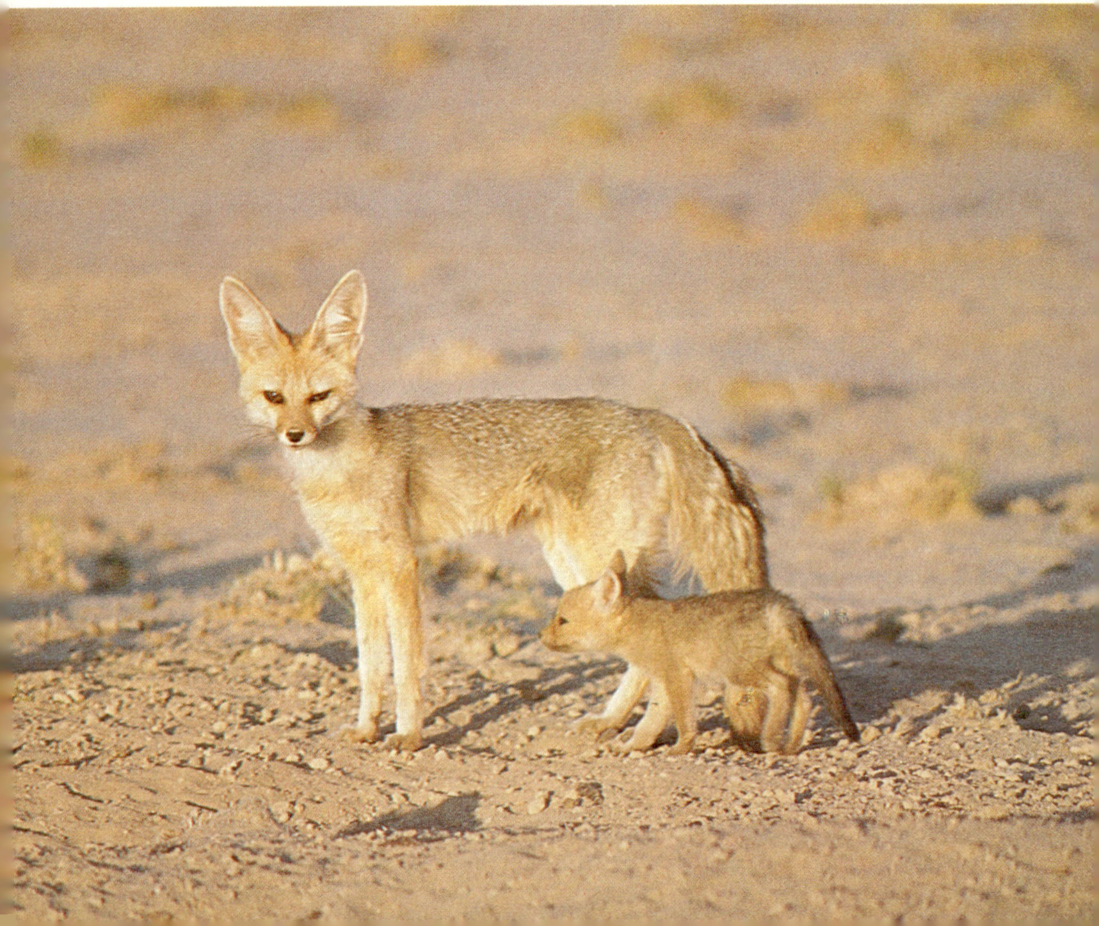

HABITS

A secretive animal, largely nocturnal, although sometimes seen in the early morning and late afternoon. Mostly solitary but sometimes seen in pairs, which might be a mother and large pup. The side-striped jackal is relatively quiet, the most common call being a harsh bark or yap. Very little else is known about this species other than that it takes refuge in thickets, holes and other suitable shelters during the day.

BREEDING

Up to six young are born per litter after a gestation period of 60–70 days. The den is often an old antbear hole.

ENEMIES AND DISEASE

Little is known about the enemies of this species, but it is likely that it would fall prey to other large predators such as lion, hyaena and leopard on occasions, and the young could be taken by large birds of prey such as the martial eagle. It is also prone to diseases which affect dogs, such as rabies and distemper.

Opposite
Top: The beautiful large brush of the Cape fox, the silvery body and reddish face are good field identification features.

Below: The Cape foxes of the Kalahari are generally paler than those from higher rainfall areas.

BLACK-BACKED JACKAL
Canis mesomelas Schreber, 1778

E: Saddle-backed jackal, silver-backed jackal. *A:* Rooijakkals

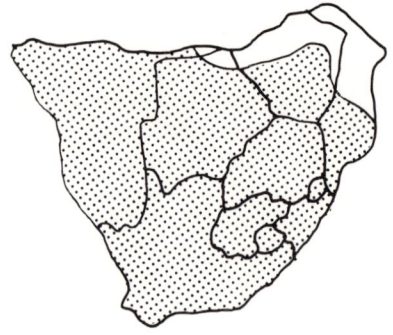

DESCRIPTION

The black-backed jackal is a medium-sized, dog-like carnivore with pointed ears which are red-brown on the back, longish black hair streaked with white on the back, and red-brown to fawn flanks and legs. The colour varies from area to area and even within one population, some individuals being pale while others are dark. The throat and underparts are pale fawn to white. The bushy tail is mostly black, 27–39 cm long, and lacks the distinct white tip of the side-striped jackal. It stands about 40 cm at the shoulder, has head and body measurements of 65–90 cm and a mass of up to 12 kg.

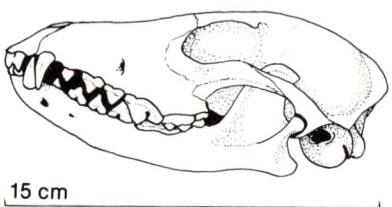

15 cm

DISTRIBUTION AND HABITAT

Widespread throughout the region except northern Zimbabwe and central and northern Mozambique, but locally extinct in places where they have come under severe hunting pressure. Less common and sometimes absent in areas where side-striped jackal occur; in the Wankie National Park, for example, the side-striped is found in the north and the black-backed in the south. The species has a wide habitat tolerance and is found from well-wooded areas through arid parts and even in coastal regions, particularly along the coast of SWA/Namibia.

Actual Size

FEEDING BEHAVIOUR

The black-backed jackal may be considered an omnivorous species because of the wide variety of food that it consumes, and this may well account for its widespread distribution. It is a well-known scavenger, feeding on morsels at lion kills and on any dead animals it may encounter. The principal food of the black-backed jackal is, however, small rodents and invertebrates (insects in particular). It also captures other live prey and has been recorded feeding on moles, dassies, hares, shrews, spring-hares, canerats, and the young of various antelopes such as blesbok, duiker, steen-bok, impala, mountain reedbuck. It may even capture some adults of the smaller antelope. It is a notorious killer of small livestock such as sheep and goats, and has in some parts been recorded killing newborn calves of domestic cows. This habit may have developed from eating the afterbirth of cows. It also feeds on a wide variety of birds, including guineafowl, korhaan, francolin and other ground birds, doves, domestic chickens and other poultry. More unusual items include porcupine, Cape grey mongoose, various lizards, geckos and snakes, earthworms, crabs, and fruit, including melons, green maize, grapes, figs, different species of 'jakkalsbessie' (*Diospyros*) and 'rosyntjiebos' or cross berry (*Grewia*). There is one record of a jackal snatching a baby baboon from a troop even though there are several records of this species 'playing' with young baboons.

HABITS

Although these animals are largely nocturnal, it is not uncommon in some areas to see them active during the day, especially in the late afternoon. They move around solitarily most of the time but may also forage in pairs. They also gather in numbers at lion kills or carcasses of large animals. The black-backed jackal is a monogamous species with a permanent pair bond. The pair defends a territory whose size depends on jackal density and the availability of food. In conservation areas territories have been found to range from 4 sq. km to 25 sq. km, and on farmland jackal have been found to range over more than 200 sq. km. The paired adults feed the young and are sometimes assisted by offspring from the previous year. Groups seen hunting together are often a mother with almost fullgrown young. Their yapping and howling calls are well known throughout Southern Africa and their chorus in the night is often the last reminder of a previous wilderness. The calls are used in communication and may be heard mainly from June to August when the females are in oestrus. These cunning animals are difficult to trap but are attracted to strong-smelling carrion. One method of killing jackals is to apply poison to such carrion set out as bait. During the day black-backed jackals rest under shady trees, or take refuge in thickets, long grass or down antbear holes which also serve as breeding dens. They can survive without water, as in the Kalahari and Namib areas, but elsewhere drink regularly.

BREEDING

Most young are born June–November with as many as eight pups in a litter, although the usual number is four. The young are born in excavations such as old antbear holes, after a gestation period of 60–70 days. They are greyish in colour at first and lack the vivid markings of the adults. Both the male and the female look after the young and will regurgitate food for them. On occasions the young from the previous litter will also feed the pups.

ENEMIES AND DISEASE

Larger predators such as lion, leopard and hyaena will kill and eat jackals occasionally, and caracals have been seen with freshly killed jackal. The remains of one was found at a bateleur eagle's nest although this may have been from a dead animal picked up by the eagle. Other large eagles such as the martial and tawny are quite capable of catching young jackal. The black-backed jackal is well known as a carrier of rabies in parts of the region and may also contract other diseases which affect dogs, such as canine distemper. At the Addo National Park in the eastern Cape many of these animals have a form of sarcoptic mange. Their main enemy is man, and many thousands of these predators have been exterminated in controlled, often on-going exercises. In most small-stock farming areas of the Cape, jackal-proof fencing has been erected on farms and the species has become rare and locally extinct. Bounties are still paid for pelts in many areas. It is unfortunate that this species will take small stock as they are otherwise a most useful animal to have on a farm. Many have also been exterminated in rabies-control operations, but despite all the persecution they are a thriving species.

CAPE FOX
Vulpes chama (A. Smith, 1833)

E: Silver fox. *A:* Draaijakkals, silwer-jakkals, silwervos

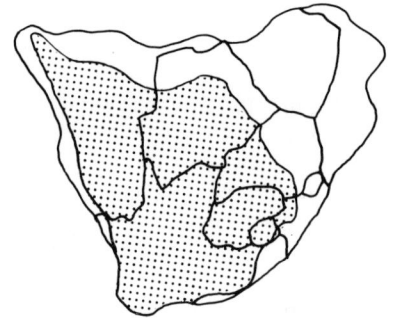

DESCRIPTION
The only true fox of Southern Africa, with a beautiful brush (tail) which is dark, long (25–40 cm) and dense. The colour of the pelt is silvery grey on the back, the legs tawny brown and the ears red-brown. The face is pointed and distinctly marked while the throat and underparts are pale fawn to white. The ears are large and pointed. Cape foxes are small animals by comparison with other members of the family, with head and body measurements of 45–62 cm, a shoulder height of about 30 cm and an adult mass of up to 4 kg.

DISTRIBUTION AND HABITAT
This species inhabits the western area of the region, from northern Botswana south through western Transvaal, western Natal, the Orange Free State to the Cape and SWA/Namibia. They appear to be more common in the short grassland, Karoo and semi-arid areas. Also found in the fynbos area of the Cape, less common or absent from well-wooded areas.

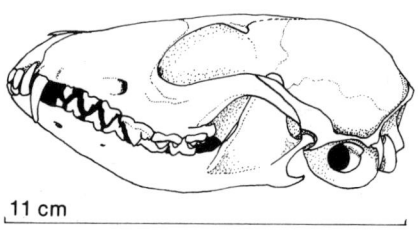

11 cm

FEEDING BEHAVIOUR
The Cape fox feeds mainly on insects, small mammals such as rodents, other invertebrates including sun spiders, and carrion. Their habit of feeding on carrion makes them vulnerable to poisoned baits, usually not intended for them. They are considered a problem in some areas by sheep farmers as they may kill and eat newborn lambs. They also feed on wild fruits, reptiles, birds and may occasionally kill animals the size of a hare. Although the canines of this species are well developed the jaw is weak and these little foxes would have difficulty in killing anything larger or stronger than a hare. On one occasion a free-ranging male was seen being chased by six large dassies.

Actual Size

Excess food is buried; a hole is dug using the front feet, the food placed inside and then covered using the nose.

HABITS

These little animals are strictly nocturnal and usually solitary but being monogamous may also be found in pairs. Though they may be flushed from thickets during the day, they dislike being active in daylight. They will also make use of antbear and springhare holes and other refuges during the day. These are not used for prolonged periods and new lairs are chosen every few weeks. They are timid animals and will arch the back and tail in a threat posture, which may be accompanied by a shrill bark. Pups use a shrill, almost bird-like call when looking for their mother while tame ones will lie down with their ears and tail flat and utter a chittering call in appeasement. They are light-footed and swift as they trot gracefully around in search of food. The ears are used a good deal when foraging and the tail or brush is curved neatly around the body for warmth when lying down. If chased by a larger animal, they will turn swiftly, swinging the tail around to confuse the pursuer.

BREEDING

Three young are the usual litter although they may number up to five. The young are born mostly during the summer months after a gestation period of about 50 days, in an old antbear hole or similar burrow. They are grey in colour with dark muzzles and tawny faces. The female may be seen lying outside the burrow during daylight hours and in areas where they are not hunted can become quite approachable. The pups can devour meat at an early age.

ENEMIES AND DISEASE

They may fall prey to larger predators and large eagles, and will also contract diseases which affect dogs, such as rabies. Many are killed on roads by vehicles and large numbers are poisoned annually in the rural areas.

BAT-EARED FOX
Otocyon megalotis (Desmarest, 1822)

A: Bakoorjakkals, bakoorvos

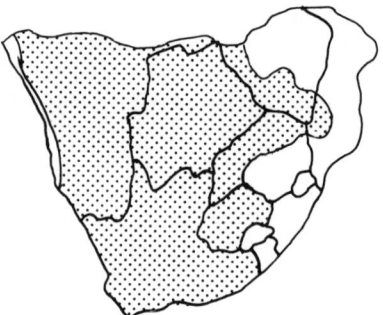

DESCRIPTION

The large, pointed dark ears and dark face of this animal are its most striking features. When lying down the ears may be flattened to make the animal less conspicuous, but when foraging they are continually moved about, often pointing forward to listen for movement on the ground. The body is long haired and silvery grey in colour, the legs are black and the tail bushy and dark. It stands about 35 cm at the shoulder but often looks larger because of its habit of walking with the back slightly arched. Adults have a mass of 3–5 kg, head and body measurements of 47–67 cm, and tail length of 23–33 cm.

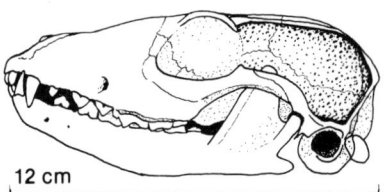

12 cm

DISTRIBUTION AND HABITAT

Widely distributed in the western and central parts of the region with a definite eastward movement in the past three or four decades. This eastward movement is evident from the Zambezi River in the north to the eastern Cape in the south. The bat-eared fox is a species of relatively open areas and it is possible that because much of the land has been degraded by livestock overgrazing, more habitat has been made available to these delightful little animals. They are fairly common in the more arid areas; in woodland regions they are more likely to occur in short grass vleis or other similar, sometimes degraded areas. The attraction may well be termites, one of their favourite food sources.

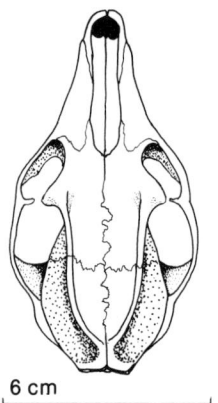

6 cm

FEEDING BEHAVIOUR

The diet of this inoffensive animal consists largely of invertebrates, particularly harvester termites which are so evident in denuded areas. It also feeds on other insects such as beetles and their larvae, small rodents, lizards, snakes, worms, scorpions, wild fruit and, more rarely, carrion. There is a

Actual Size

record of a group attacking a steenbok in a trap but this must be considered most unusual. The method of locating prey is by moving about with ears pointed towards the ground, often swinging the head from side to side to listen for sounds which might indicate something edible. The exact locality of prey is determined with the ears pointed forward and the nose held close to the ground. If the food source is hidden, then the fox will dig rapidly with the front feet.

HABITS

The bat-eared fox is a gregarious species which may be seen in groups of up to 12 while out foraging. They are essentially nocturnal but may move about in the late morning and early evening in areas where they are not disturbed while in the Kalahari they are predominantly diurnal during winter. During the day they take refuge in bushes, thickets, long grass and old antbear holes. Although relatively silent their call has been described as a rather shrill repetitive 'who-who-who'. Both the male and the female mark objects with a small deposit of urine.

BREEDING

Up to six young are born after a gestation period of around 60 days in holes excavated by the parents. As with a number of other carnivores, these holes are often old ant-bear holes which have been modifed by the foxes. They dig readily and will excavate their own holes if necesary, with several entrances, exits and chambers. The new-born young are grey in colour with a slight reddish line along the back. They accompany both adults once out of the burrow and may be seen exploring near the entrance of the den when only three to four weeks old. Breeding appears to take place in the summer months.

ENEMIES AND DISEASE

They may fall prey to larger predators and the young are small enough to be caught by large birds of prey. They are also prone to diseases that affect dogs, such as rabies. Sometimes killed on the roads by vehicles, and often innocent victims of problem animal control exercises.

AFRICAN WILD DOG
Lycaon pictus (Temminck, 1820)

E: Cape hunting dog. *A:* Wildehond

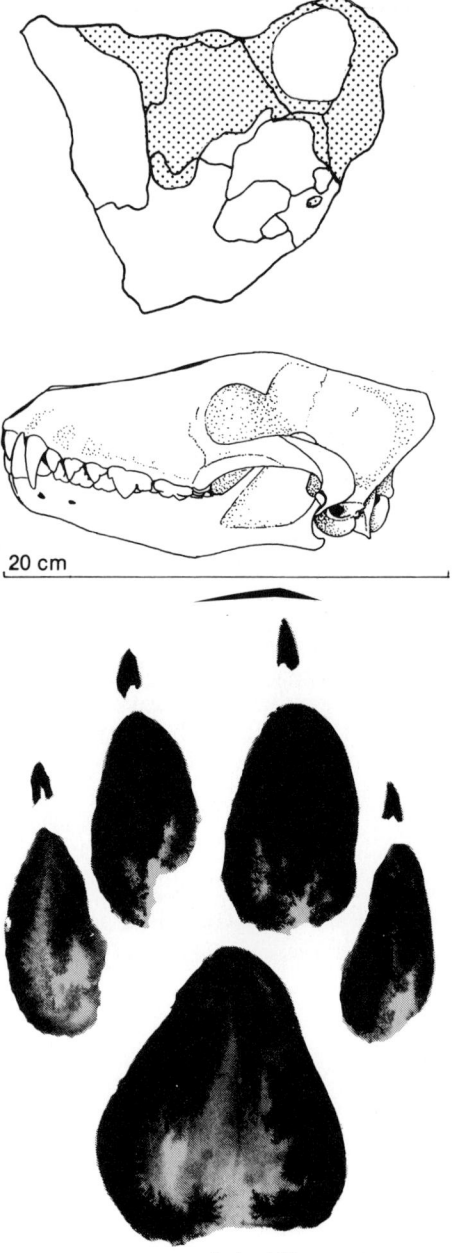

20 cm

Actual Size

DESCRIPTION

A striking feature of the wild dog is the marbled colour pattern of the short, coarse coat which is made up of irregular blotches of black, brown, white and buffy-yellow so that no two individuals look exactly alike. It has a black face with a distinctive black stripe running from the nose to the top of the large head, which contrasts strongly with the pale sandy colour of the forehead and cheeks and the conspicuous ruff of dark brown to dull orange hair at the throat. The ears are large, rounded and black, the muzzle short and broad. The body is slender, the legs long and thin and almost all hunting dogs have white-tipped tails — only rarely is a dark tail seen. It stands 60–78 cm at the shoulder, has head and body measurements of 76–112 cm and the bushy tail may be 30–40 cm long. Adults weigh 20–30 kg. There are no marked differences in appearance between the sexes, though the dogs are larger than bitches. Wild dogs have a strong, musky odour.

DISTRIBUTION AND HABITAT

The species has been exterminated over most of its natural range and is today probably the rarest carnivore on the subcontinent. Wild dogs still occupy diverse habitats from arid shrub grassland to moister savanna and woodlands. Their habitat choice has been found to be influenced by available game concentrations, water, and competition from other large predators. Where lions and spotted hyaena are abundant, as in the central district of the Kruger Park, wild dogs are rare, though in all other respects the habitat is ideal.

Opposite: Bat-eared foxes usually forage in groups; the large ears are pointed forwards to pick up sounds of their prey, which consists mostly of termites.

Wild dogs occur only sparsely, if at all, in the north-eastern parts of SWA/Namibia; they are widespread in Botswana except in the more closely settled and developed eastern parts; they still occur in the remoter parts of Zimbabwe and Mozambique. They are extinct in South Africa except for the vagrants which occasionally appear in the Kalahari Gemsbok National Park from Botswana, the good populations in the Kruger National Park and some adjoining areas — on cattle ranches in the lowveld they are destroyed as vermin. A small population has been established in the Hluhluwe/Umfolozi game reserve complex.

FEEDING BEHAVIOUR

Wild dog packs kill a wide range of small to medium-sized animals such as oribi, steenbok, duiker, bushbuck, reedbuck, springbok and warthog. In the savanna and woodland areas of the Kruger Park their preference is for impala which make up 93% of their diet. They are able to kill animals much larger than themselves, but normally would take only the young or females of kudu, waterbuck, wildebeest, eland, tsessebe, giraffe, buffalo, sable, lechwe, hartebeest and nyala. Smaller creatures like hares, canerats and other rodents and birds are also taken, and more unusual items recorded include young lion and honey badger. Wild dogs hunt co-operatively, depending on speeds of up to 50 k.p.h. and stamina for running down their prey. While doing so, they bite and tear at the flanks and buttocks of the victim and may even swallow chunks of meat while the prey is still alive. This biting is very likely aided by the jagged edges which their cheek teeth have — a feature not shared by the other members of the family. Eventually the prey stumbles and falls and is then rapidly torn apart and killed. As soon as the prey falls, the dogs at the kill and subsequent arrivals lift their tails in the air, showing off the white tip as a signal to others in the pack that the kill has been made. An adult impala ram was torn apart and almost entirely consumed by a pack of eight dogs in only two minutes. Skin, heads, bones, fat and entrails are usually left at the site of the kill. The dogs bolt the meat and, when they have pups to feed, return to the den where they regurgitate food for them. They will also regurgitate meat for adults that might have stayed at the den, such as lame animals or adults guarding pups. Packs hunt twice a day, usually in the early morning and late afternoon and also at night on occasion. Hunting dogs have been recorded taking carrion, but only rarely. Hunts are not always successful and small packs are easily deterred by a determined zebra stallion using hooves and teeth. Wild dogs are silent while hunting; communication is by sight and smell. Typically, they jump up and down, and rear up on their hind legs to see over the grass. They drink regularly, usually after the morning and before the evening hunt. Wild dogs are usually unwilling to enter deep water — and there are many records of antelope escaping from them by swimming across a river.

There are no records of wild dogs killing man, but they do take domestic stock. Their method of killing had traditionally been

---

Opposite
Top: The irregular, marbled colour pattern, the black face with black mid-facial stripe and rounded ears are characteristic of the African wild dog.

Centre: The remains of an impala, killed by wild dogs, showing how the meat has been ripped off.

Below: The wild dog has distinctive jagged edges to the cheek teeth and these help in tearing the meat off its prey.

regarded as cruel, but it is difficult to justify such a view: the victims are in a state of shock and excitement and probably experience less suffering than an animal being drowned by a crocodile or suffocated by a lion.

HABITS

Wild dogs are intensely social animals, living in packs of 6–30 animals which are predominantly males. All food is shared equally among members of the pack. Usually only one bitch at a time has pups and all members of the pack help to feed them. There is apparently no leader and relatively little aggression occurs between pack members. The pack is nomadic and may wander over areas as large as 500–2000 sq. km unless they have pups; in the latter case they confine their hunting activities to an area within easy reach of the den.

Except when engaged in a hunt, wild dogs can be very vocal — uttering a lively twittering or chirping call for greeting and whines and yelps when excited. They also make a mournful hooting call, usually heard at night, and often used by a lost dog trying to contact the pack. This call is seldom used during the day when dogs depend on sight to maintain contact. When alarmed they utter a hoarse bark.

Wild dogs engage in an elaborate greeting ceremony, which involves much cringing, mouthing, nuzzling and dashing around in circles. This behaviour serves to rouse and excite members of a pack after a rest period and so prepare them for a hunt. They rest during the heat of the day and seem to prefer deep shade. During rain they shelter under thickets and huddle together for warmth and protection. Wild dogs display no fear of vehicles, usually ignoring them. Consequently, they are easily approached and shot.

BREEDING

Usually only one bitch in the pack comes into oestrus and she is mated by the dominant male. Gestation lasts for 60–72 days, and a litter of 2–6 pups are born which are blind and almost naked. As many as 16 pups have been recorded in a litter but this is unusual. They suckle for up to three months but are also fed on regurgitated meat from about three weeks. The pups spend their first three months in and around the den in which they were born, which is usually an antbear burrow. Thereafter they start moving out with the adults to hunt. During this period the adults let the young feed first at a kill. Soon after the pack once more becomes nomadic. Wild dogs are seasonal breeders, most young are born April–June. As game is usually concentrated near water during this time, conditions are most suitable for the adults to operate in a smaller range around the pupping den.

ENEMIES AND DISEASE

Hunting dogs are well able to defend themselves against other predators, and in addition they can always depend on their speed to get away. They are, however, occasionally killed by lions and leopards. Their kills are sometimes stolen by lions and, if there are enough of them to intimidate the dogs, also by spotted hyaenas.

Wild dogs are susceptible to rickets, mange, abortion caused by *Brucella abortus* and canine distemper, but there is no good information on how important such diseases may be in depressing a wild dog population. Declines in wild dog populations in the Kruger Park in past years have been linked to disease conditions and in East Africa to disease and to an increase in spotted hyaena numbers. Their greatest enemy in modern times has, however, been man, who has ruthlessly exterminated the species over most of its range.

POLECATS, WEASELS, HONEY BADGER, OTTERS

FAMILY MUSTELIDAE

The mustelids are short-legged and fairly long-bodied carnivores, some of which have well-developed scent glands. The teeth are slightly reduced and specialised while the cranium (brain case) is large. Most members make remarkably intelligent pets. They vary greatly in size and are represented by five species in the region: the striped polecat, white-naped weasel, honey badger, clawless otter and spotted-necked otter.

STRIPED POLECAT
Ictonyx striatus Perry, 1810

E: Zorilla, skunk. *A:* Stinkmuishond

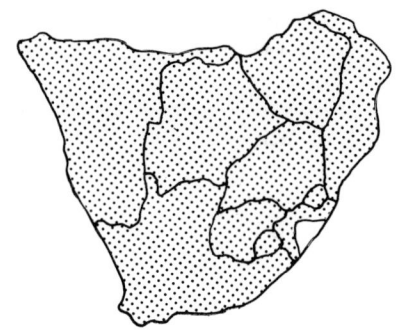

DESCRIPTION

The striped polecat is a small long-haired carnivore with four distinct white stripes running along its back from the crown of the head to the tail; the body is shiny black in colour except for a white patch on the forehead and a white patch behind each eye. The base of the tail is black with the rest usually white although this is very variable even in the same population. The polecat is a squat animal compared to the next species with which it is sometimes confused. The body is about 35 cm long in adults, the tail about 20 cm long and the shoulder height of about 10-14 cm. Females are slightly smaller than males, their body mass being up to 800 g and 1200 g respectively.

DISTRIBUTION AND HABITAT

This species is widespread throughout the sub-continent with a very wide habitat tolerance. They are common in many of the more open areas such as the Karoo and highveld grasslands, and may be absent from moist coastal forests.

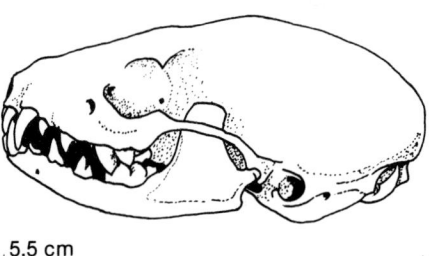

5,5 cm

FEEDING BEHAVIOUR

These little carnivores feed mainly on insects and small rodents, many of which are located by scratching around with the sharp claws on the front feet. They also feed on lizards, snakes, frogs, small birds, the eggs of some ground nesting birds, moles, invertebrates including sun spiders, spiders, worms, larvae of dungbeetles, scorpions, centipedes and grasshoppers. The food is finely masticated by the action of the cheek teeth. The eyes and nose are continually in use when searching for food.

Actual Size

HABITS

This species is strictly nocturnal and lives solitarily in burrows among rocks or in hollow tree stumps. They are well known for their threat posture with the tail held high, back arched and hair erect. As a last resort they will squirt foul-smelling liquid from the anal glands at an intruder and this odour may persist for days afterwards. In this behaviour pattern the tail is curled over the back, the head tucked in and the anal region pointed towards the source of danger. They do, however, make delightful pets and rarely resort to using the anal glands when tame. The calls are difficult to describe but vary from those used in greeting, to defence, threat and distress, the latter being high-pitched and unpleasant to the ear.

BREEDING

One to three young are born in a suitable den after a gestation period of about 36 days. At birth they are pink and hairless with closed eyes, the colour pattern only becoming evident at about one week old. The eyes open at about 40 days and adult size is reached in about 20 weeks. The young may accompany the mother from about two months of age and are sometimes carried along by the scruff of the neck. Breeding takes place during spring and summer.

ENEMIES AND DISEASE

Many of these little predators are killed on the roads, especially along some of the main highways in rural areas. They have also been recorded as food items of large birds of prey including bateleur, crowned eagle, martial eagle and giant eagle owl, although these may have been road casualties in some cases in view of the nocturnal nature of the species. They may also be killed by larger predators and are susceptible to rabies. In some areas they have been found to be carrying numerous ectoparasites (ticks, fleas).

WHITE-NAPED WEASEL
Poecilogale albinucha (Gray, 1864)

E: African weasel, striped weasel.
A: Slangmuishond

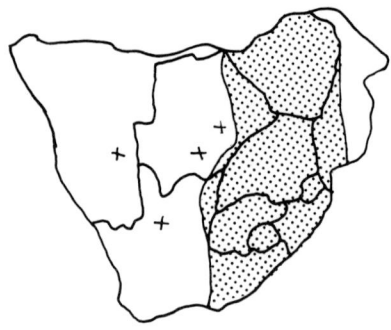

DESCRIPTION

This is a slender animal, sometimes confused with the striped polecat. Although the body is short-haired, the tail by comparison is quite bushy. The overall colour is black, with four dirty white to yellowish stripes running from the head where they form a distinct cap, to a white tail. It is about 28–35 cm long with a tail 14–18 cm long and a body mass of up to 380 g in males and 290 g in the females. It is distinguished from the previous species by the small size, elongated slender body, short body hair, and white cap on the head.

DISTRIBUTION AND HABITAT

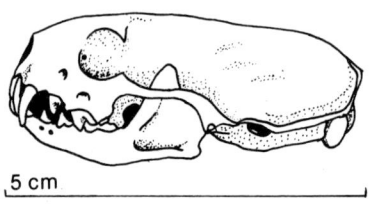

5 cm

The elusive nature of this small carnivore does little towards establishing its true distribution, but it appears to be quite widespread in the entire eastern half of the region. It also appears to have a wide habitat tolerance within its distribution and may be found in the drier parts of the Karoo in the eastern Cape to the more moist savanna areas of eastern Zimbabwe. Distribution and status in Mozambique are uncertain.

Actual Size

FEEDING BEHAVIOUR

The main food source in the wild is probably small rodents. A captive specimen in Natal is said to have ignored eggs, snakes, lizards and various invertebrates. Captive animals are, however, very good small rodent killers and the body shape certainly suggests a somewhat underground existence which would enable the animal to get to golden moles, molerats and other small rodents living in underground burrows. Their eyesight appears to be poor and they probably detect prey by smell, which would be a useful adaption for hunting underground. They evidently kill small rodents by biting them at the back of the head, then twisting the slender body around the prey to hold it securely.

HABITS

These interesting animals are predominantly nocturnal, although there are records of them being active during daylight. They are generally solitary but family groups of as many as four have been seen, consisting of a female with young. In such instances the adult walks in front with the young following nose to tail. They sleep in a coiled-up position in dens which may be a burrow in the ground, a hollow log or a crevice in rocks.

Holes are excavated by using the digging claws on the front feet. In captivity they use dung middens, but this is often a feature of captive carnivores and does not necessarily apply in the wild. The calls have been described as a quiet growl, higher-pitched growls in rapid succession, a sharp half-bark/half-scream, grunting and snorting quietly, and a rapid 'chur-churr-churr-churr' by a male when confronted by a female. In serious threat or distress the hair on the tail is erected, a loud bark/scream is emitted and a foul-smelling liquid may be secreted from the anal glands.

BREEDING

The young are born hairless and pink after a gestation period of 32 days and the litters number from one to three individuals. The eyes are closed at birth and open at about 52 days. They are said to be able to kill small animals at 13 weeks of age.

ENEMIES AND DISEASE

Virtually nothing is recorded on the enemies and diseases of these animals. They may well be killed by larger predators and birds of prey when encountered.

HONEY BADGER
Mellivora capensis (Schreber, 1776)

A: Ratel

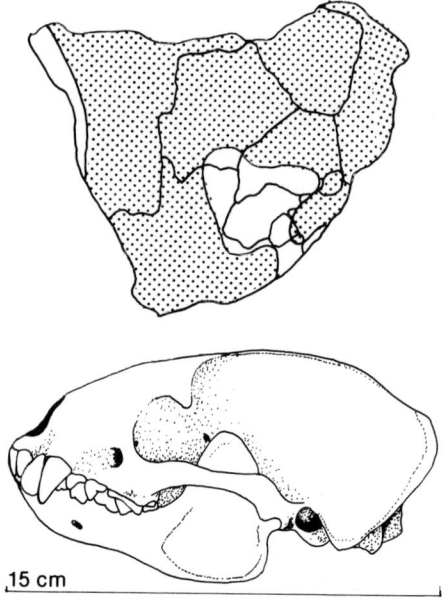

DESCRIPTION

The honey badger is squat and stocky with powerful legs, a thick neck, no external ear-lobes, a short tail, coarse hair and small beady eyes. The upper part of the body is grey to white and the lower part, including the face, dark brown to black with the lighter-coloured skin showing through areas with a sparse hair covering. The skin is thick and tough, and the front feet have large curved claws. It has a shoulder height of around 30 cm and a body mass of up to 13 kg, head and body measurements of 50–90 cm, and a 16–19 cm long tail. It cannot be mistaken for any other carnivore in the region.

15 cm

DISTRIBUTION AND HABITAT

This species has a patchy but fairly wide-spread distribution and is rare in many parts of its range. They are absent in many areas where they formerly occurred. They have a wide habitat tolerance and may be found from the moist coastal forests of Knysna to the hot, arid Kalahari.

FEEDING BEHAVIOUR

These animals are fairly omnivorous by nature and a wide variety of food items have been recorded. There appears to be an association between honey badgers and a bird known as the honeyguide which feeds on bee larvae among other things. These birds lure humans to beehives with their call and it is said that the badgers will also respond to their calls. In the Kalahari chanting goshawks and black-backed jackals are

Actual Size

Opposite
Top: A low-intensity threat by a foraging striped polecat involves only a slight lifting of the tail.

Below: The long slender body of the white-naped weasel is ideally shaped for manoeuvring in rodent holes and tunnels.

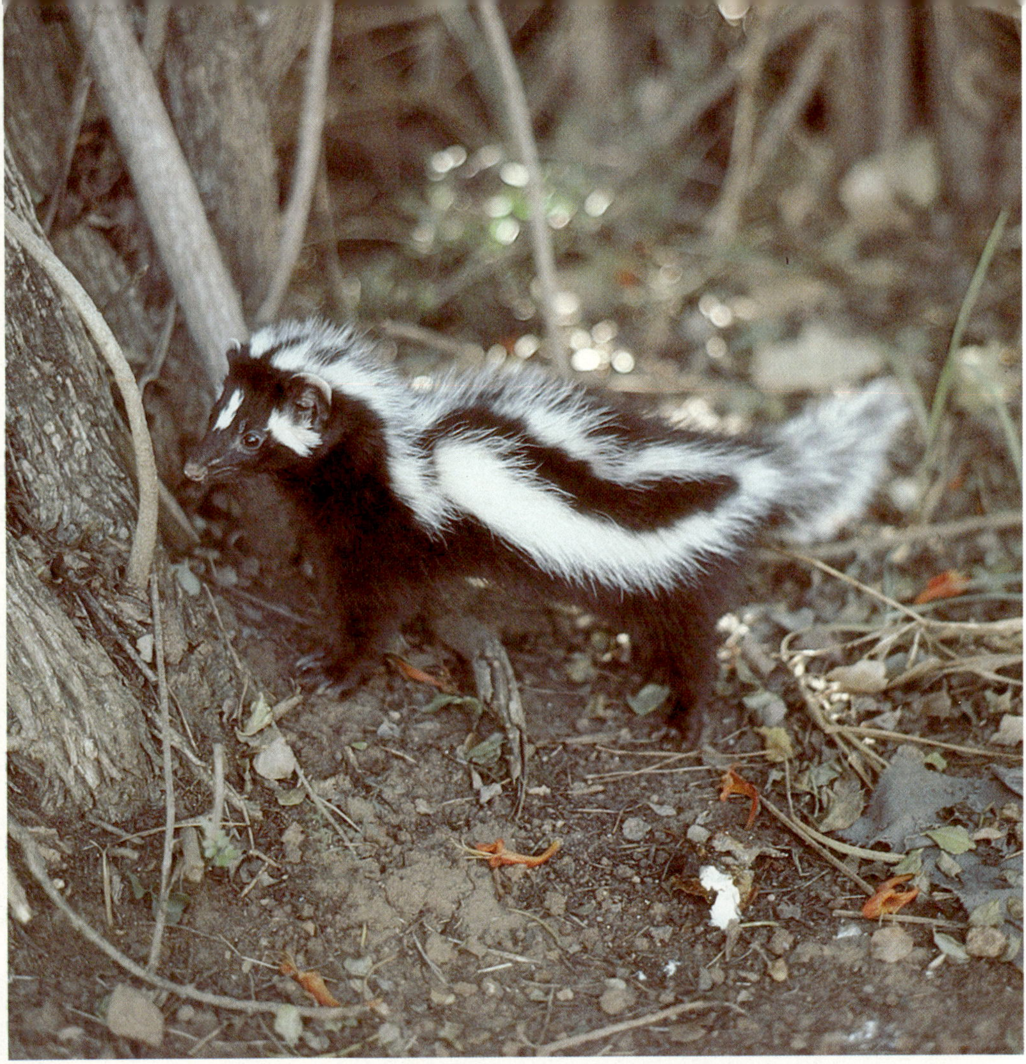
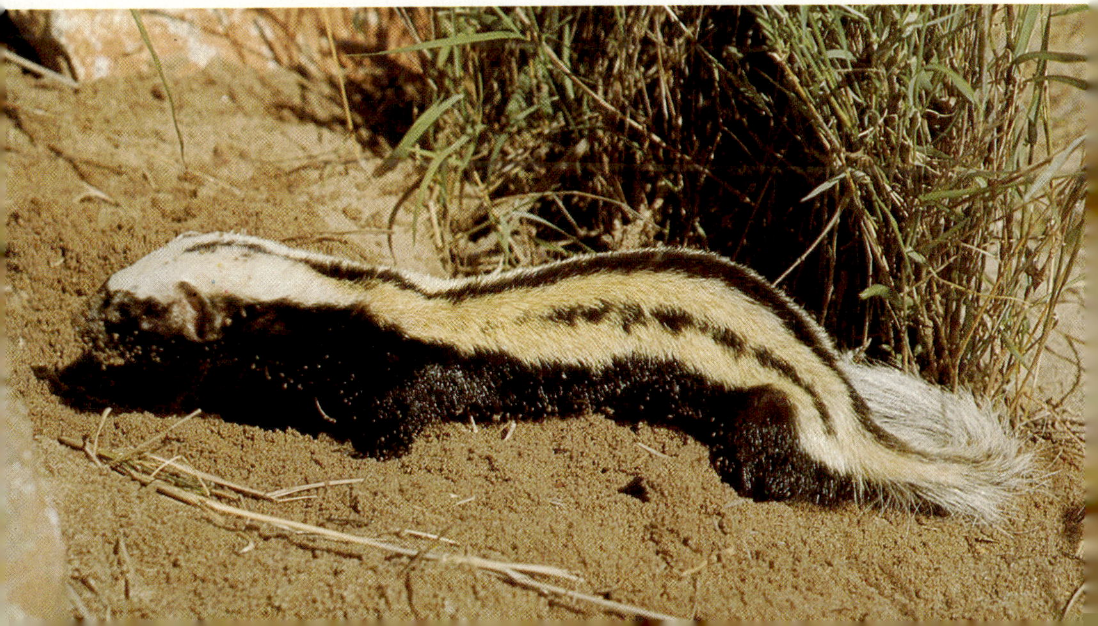

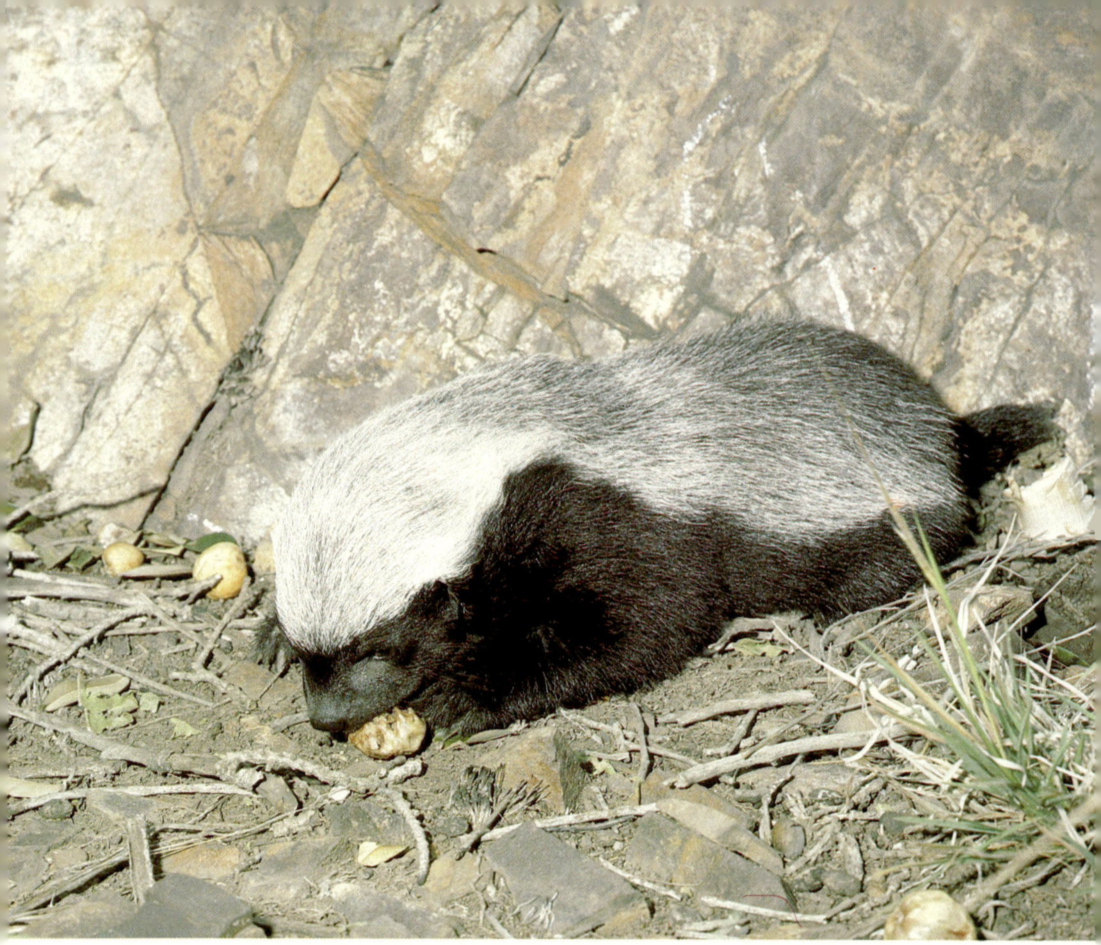

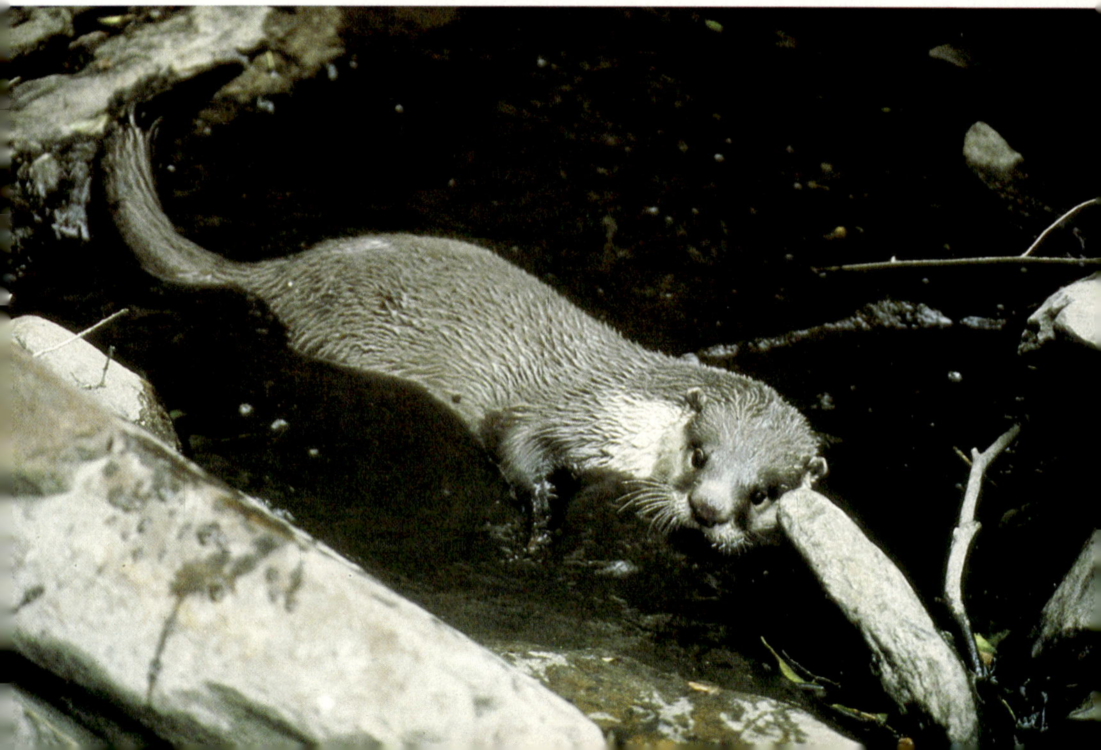

often associated with foraging honey badgers, when they catch the small rodents that escape after being dug up by the ratel. The long powerful nails on the front feet are used for digging, ripping bark from trees, and turning over logs and stones and other objects in search of food. These claws can also be used for climbing and one was seen to use them in clawing a leguaan out of a tree. Apart from honey and bee larvae, these tenacious animals feed on small rodents, reptiles, invertebrates, fish from drying pools, roots, bulbs, fruit, birds including poultry, and a variety of mammals such as water mongoose, porcupines and young antelope. They will also scavenge around dwellings, picking up scraps of food, emptying dustbins and even, in one case, breaking into a skin shed. There is a record of one killing a three-metre python in the Kruger National Park.

HABITS

The honey badger is probably best known for its aggressive nature, tenacity and toughness. They are formidable opponents for any attacker and dogs are no match for them. The skin is tough and the long nails are used to scrape attackers away from the throat after which they are bitten in the face with sharp teeth and powerful jaws. Honey badgers are recorded as standing back for no animal: they are reputed to have been observed chasing an elephant away from a waterhole and killing animals as big as buffalo by biting off their testicles and leaving them to bleed to death. In the Matopos (Zimbabwe) an irate honey badger, which had several porcupine quills stuck in it, met up with a tractor which it promptly attacked. They tend to waddle along rather than walk, and may stop periodically with the body flat on the ground and head raised. They are generally solitary animals, but may occur in family groups of up to four in number. They are nocturnal to a large extent, but may be seen foraging during the day in areas where they are not disturbed. During the day they take refuge in suitable sites such as antbear holes, which sometimes have the strong musk odour of this species. The calls vary from a growl to a grunt to a high-pitched scream of annoyance. When riled they may fly into a state of blind aggression during which time a strong musk may be produced. This musk is also produced, however, during times of contentment. The honey badger also makes a low-pitched rattling call (hence the name ratel), utters a 'h-r-r-r-r' grating sound when foraging and a 'harr' call when annoyed. They are said to enjoy wallowing in mud. Despite their aggressive nature, they have been known to make delightful pets.

BREEDING

Two to three young are born after a gestation period of some 180 days, but little information is available. The young are born in an underground lair and are quite dark coloured at birth.

ENEMIES AND DISEASE

A number are destroyed in farming areas because of poultry theft by the species, and some fall victim to problem animal control practices. Cases of rabies in this species are rare.

Opposite
Top: A young honey badger shows the stocky build and contrasting grey-white and black colouring of the adult.

Below: Small ears, a snub nose and long whiskers are typical of the clawless otter, here seen foraging in the dark waters of a forest pool.

CLAWLESS OTTER
Aonyx capensis (Schinz, 1821)

E: Cape clawless otter. *A:* Groot otter

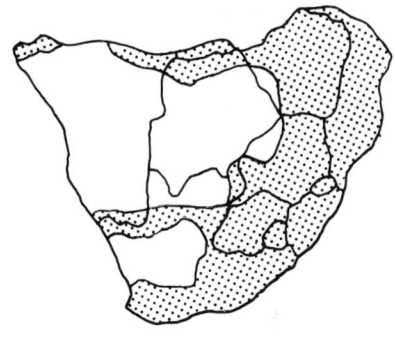

DESCRIPTION

This animal has a beautiful soft, dark brown coat with pale yellow to white fur on the lower part of the face and chest. It has a snub nose with long whiskers protruding on either side of the face. The ears are small, the tail heavy at the base and pointed with short fur, while the nails on the toes are very small giving a clawless appearance. Unlike the next species, the toes are not webbed. The body mass is up to 22 kg and the body shape quite seal-like, 73–88 cm long with a 46–51 cm long tail.

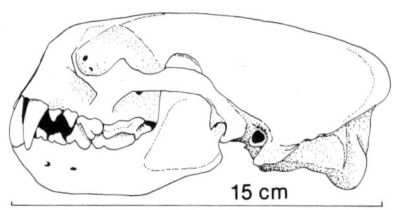

15 cm

DISTRIBUTION AND HABITAT

This species is dependent on the presence of water and is widely distributed except in the more arid areas of the west, south-west and central parts of the region. Although temporary pools are sometimes made use of, the presence of permanent water is essential. Clawless otters also occur along the coast and will swim and forage in the sea, but require the terrestrial cover and habitat in general for survival.

FEEDING BEHAVIOUR

Crabs (marine and freshwater) form the main part of their diet and the undigested remains of these feature prominently in their dung, which is deposited in conspicuous middens. The dung deposits and middens of the water mongoose are very similar but much smaller, the droppings of the otter being about 4 cm in diameter. Other food items include fish, frogs, invertebrates, birds (including waterfowl and poultry), molluscs, reptiles (including leguaans and snakes) and various small mammals. They have been known to take carrion. When feeding on freshwater mussels they will use objects such as rocks, old bottles and tree stumps to crack the shells, much in the same way as a mon-

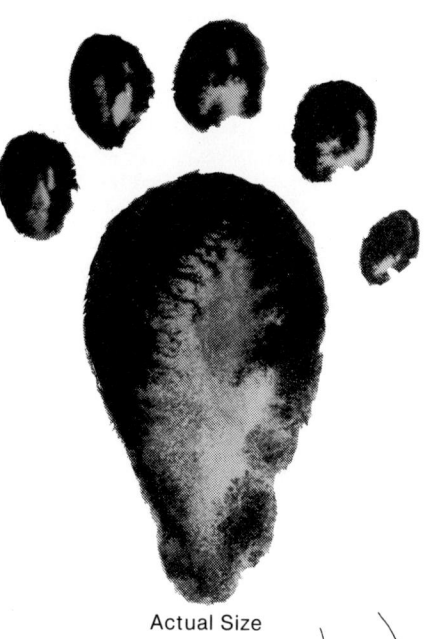

Actual Size

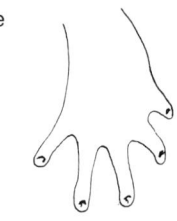

goose. When foraging the front feet are used extensively to feel under rocks for prey such as crabs and frogs and they are also adept at turning over small rocks. They are good swimmers and are able to catch slow-moving fish. In the sea they feed on shellfish, fish, crabs, lobsters and octopus.

HABITS

The otter is at home in the water and somewhat clumsy on land; nevertheless, it does wander around quite extensively in search of feeding areas, especially during the rains. The clawless otter is not, however, as aquatic as the next species. It is predominantly nocturnal but in captivity becomes quite diurnal in habit. Being playful creatures, they make good pets but have a vicious bite. Rolling places and slides down river banks are common signs of their presence and the fortunate observer may see their playful antics early in the morning in secluded areas. They are fairly gregarious and may be encountered in family groups of up to five individuals. Much of the daylight hours is spent in the shelter of thick undergrowth on a riverbank, holes under large trees next to the water, rock crevices or similar refuges. They are strong swimmers and are quite at home in the powerful currents of the Zambezi River. Their calls vary a great deal and include growls, whines, hisses and squeaks.

BREEDING

Two to three young are born in a den after a gestation period of some 60–65 days, usually during the summer months. Young are sometimes left on the river bank while the adult forages nearby, and when very young they show little concern when approached.

ENEMIES AND DISEASE

Small numbers are destroyed while raiding poultry and others are killed when suspected of depleting fish stocks. They would be killed by large carnivores if the opportunity arose and in places where crocodiles and otters occur together, there is every possibility that these large reptiles would take the odd one. Little is known about their diseases.

SPOTTED-NECKED OTTER
Lutra maculicollis (Lichtenstein, 1835)

A: Klein otter

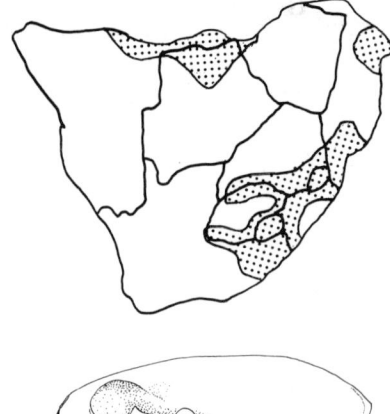

DESCRIPTION

A smaller otter than the previous species with a mass of up to 9 kg, head and body measurements of 46–75 cm, and a tail measuring 30–50 cm. These animals are a soft dark brown to chestnut colour with pale-coloured throat and undersides. The chest is buffy with large dark spots. Unlike the previous species, the feet of the spotted-necked otter are webbed and have a distinct nail on each toe.

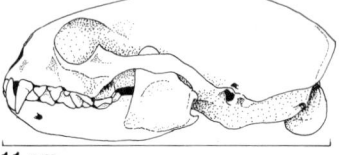

11 cm

DISTRIBUTION AND HABITAT

Occurs in the upper Zambezi system of northern Botswana, absent from Zimbabwe; then found again from the eastern Cape, through western Natal northwards to southern Mozambique. Also recorded near the Zambezi delta in Mozambique. There appear to be at least two fairly distinct populations and the status of the species in parts is uncertain. A more aquatic species than the previous one, it is confined to areas with permanent water and shows a preference for deeper and calmer water.

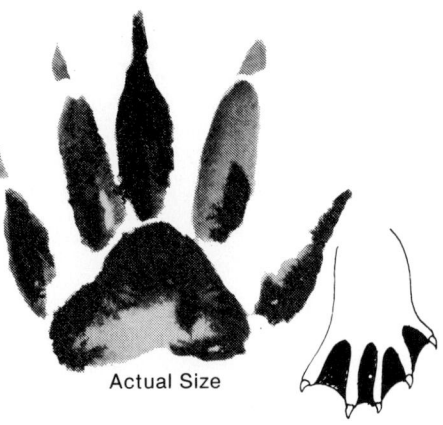

Actual Size

FEEDING BEHAVIOUR

This species appears to prefer fish but also feeds fairly extensively on crabs and frogs, including the common platanna or clawed toad. The diet also includes invertebrates and birds. The spotted-necked otter apparently hunts by day and captures its prey with the mouth, generally taking items to the shore to feed. By contrast, the clawless otter captures most of its prey with the feet and will eat most of what is caught in the water, unless the items are large, such as waterfowl and large fish, or need cracking as in the case of large freshwater mussels.

HABITS

Little is known about spotted-necked otters, but they appear to be diurnal in most

places. They also have conspicuous latrines and rolling places near the water, and are quite gregarious, occurring in parties of up to five. Generally a shy and elusive creature.

BREEDING

One to three young are born but information is lacking.

ENEMIES AND DISEASE

As with the previous species, these animals would probably fall prey to large predators and crocodiles on occasion. No further information available.

CIVET, GENETS, MONGOOSES, SURICATE

FAMILY VIVERRIDAE

This family includes a variety of small to medium-sized carnivores which have short legs and long bodies, often with a bushy tail. Nearly all have active scent or anal glands which secrete strong-smelling substances. Unlike the cats, they have non-retractile claws (except the genets), more teeth and long faces. They are also usually the most abundant group of carnivores in most areas. In Southern Africa there are two species of civet, two genets and 12 species of mongoose.

AFRICAN CIVET
Civettictis civetta Schreber, 1776

E: Civet. *A:* Siwetkat, siwet

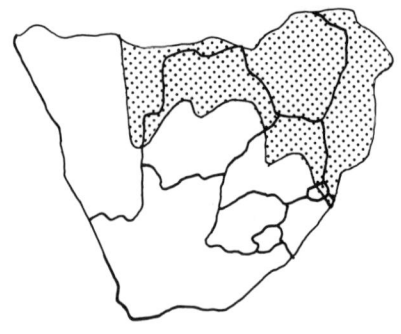

DESCRIPTION

A large, stocky member of the family with a mass of about 18 kg and a shoulder height of 40 cm. It is a dark animal with black legs and black blotches on a silvery grey background on the rest of the body. The face has a distinct black mask while the muzzle is white, the nose is black and the forehead is speckled grey. The ears are relatively small and rounded and there is a conspicuous white mark running down the side of the neck above the black throat. A prominent ridge of black hair runs along the line of the back into the tail. Head and body measures 68–89 cm and the tail about 45 cm.

DISTRIBUTION AND HABITAT

This animal is widespread in Zimbabwe, northern Botswana, north-eastern SWA/ Namibia, northern and eastern Transvaal, Swaziland, northern Natal and Mozambique. They favour the better-watered areas but are found in a variety of habitats and appear to be more common in open woodland and savanna areas.

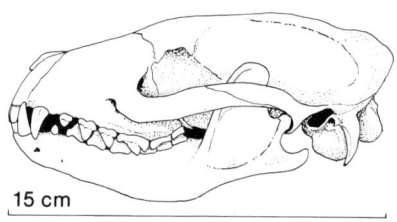

15 cm

FEEDING BEHAVIOUR

Probably the most omnivorous of our carnivores, they feed on a great range of items including carrion. Their diet consists of snakes, lizards, birds and their eggs, invertebrates such as insects, millipedes, scorpions and sun spiders, larvae of beetles, rodents, frogs, carrion of most kinds, and a great variety of fruit. Dung samples have been found to contain silver paper and old rags, probably as a result of scavenging around human habitation. Foraging is usually a very active process of moving about sniffing and digging.

Actual Size

HABITS

The African civet is nocturnal and may be found singly or in pairs. When disturbed they sound a warning bark, and when threatened erect the mane and growl deeply. These animals have a habit of depositing their dung in large, well-used latrines or middens (also known as civetries), the actual droppings in some cases being enormous in comparison to the size of the animal, measuring up to 25 cm long and 5 cm in diameter. The anal (or perineal) glands secrete a substance known as 'civet' which has for centuries been used in the manufacture of perfume. The secretion is usually collected from caged animals by using a spatula. In the wild the secretion is deposited on trees, rocks, shrubs and herbs as a means of advertising the presence of an individual in a home range. Tree trunks are normally used and marked about 35 cm above the ground.

BREEDING

Up to four young are born in a secluded lair during the summer months after a gestation of about 60 days. They are weaned at about five months.

ENEMIES AND DISEASE

This species will at times fall prey to large carnivores. One was once found freshly killed by a leopard but uneaten. The young are also taken by large birds of prey such as the Cape eagle owl. Little is known about the diseases that affect the species.

PALM CIVET
Nandinia binotata (Reinwardt, 1830)

E: Tree civet, two-spotted palm civet. *A:*
Palmsiwet, boomsiwet

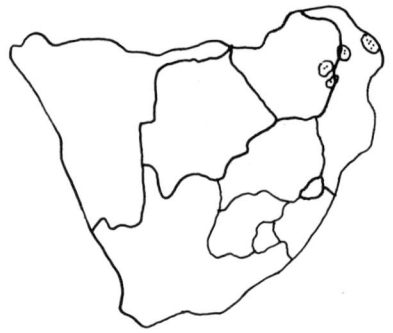

DESCRIPTION

This species has a buffy coat tinged with
brown, with scattered brown to dark brown
spots on the body which form rings around
the tail. There are two cream-coloured
spots on the shoulders, hence the alterna-
tive name of 'two-spotted palm civet'. The
body is stocky, the ears small, the head
rounded and the tail long. The legs are short
and the toes have sharp claws adapted for
climbing. The body mass is about 2,5 kg in
adults, head and body about 51 cm long and
the tail about 58 cm.

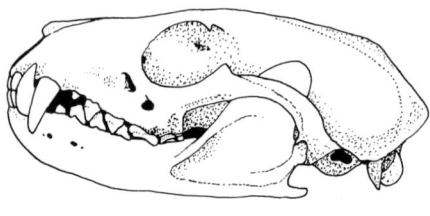

DISTRIBUTION AND HABITAT

These animals are rare in the region,
occurring in isolated pockets in the evergreen forests of eastern Zimbabwe and in
Mozambique. Further north they occur in
equatorial forests and are associated with
palm trees.

10 cm

FEEDING BEHAVIOUR

They feed on vegetable matter, mainly
fruit, but also including leaves. They also
take small rodents, fruit bats, birds, eggs
and insects. They probably eat the fruit of
palm trees, and hence their association.

HABITS

Very little is known about this species.
They are arboreal and nocturnal, hiding in
thickets and vines during the day. They

Hind Foot
Actual Size

Opposite: The spotted-necked otter has characteristic pale spotting on the throat and
conspicuous claws.

Overleaf: The conspicuous black band across the face and white muzzle are striking facial
features of the African civet.

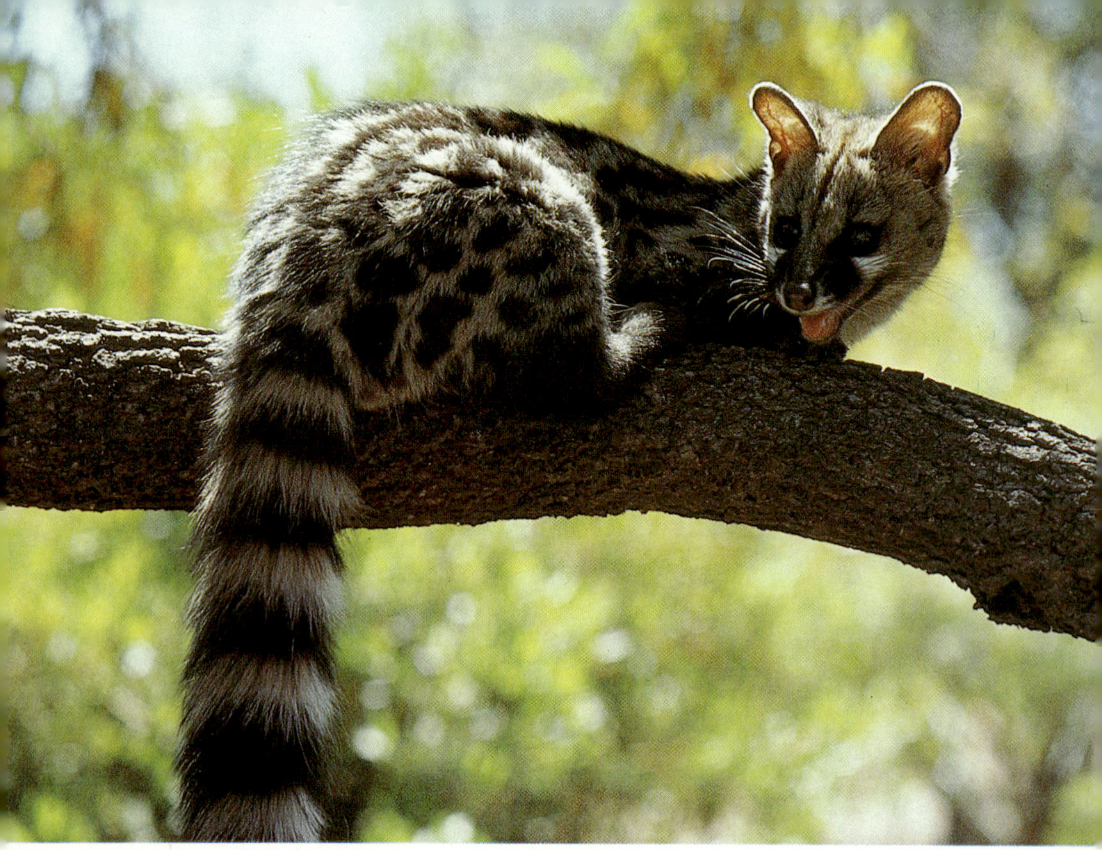

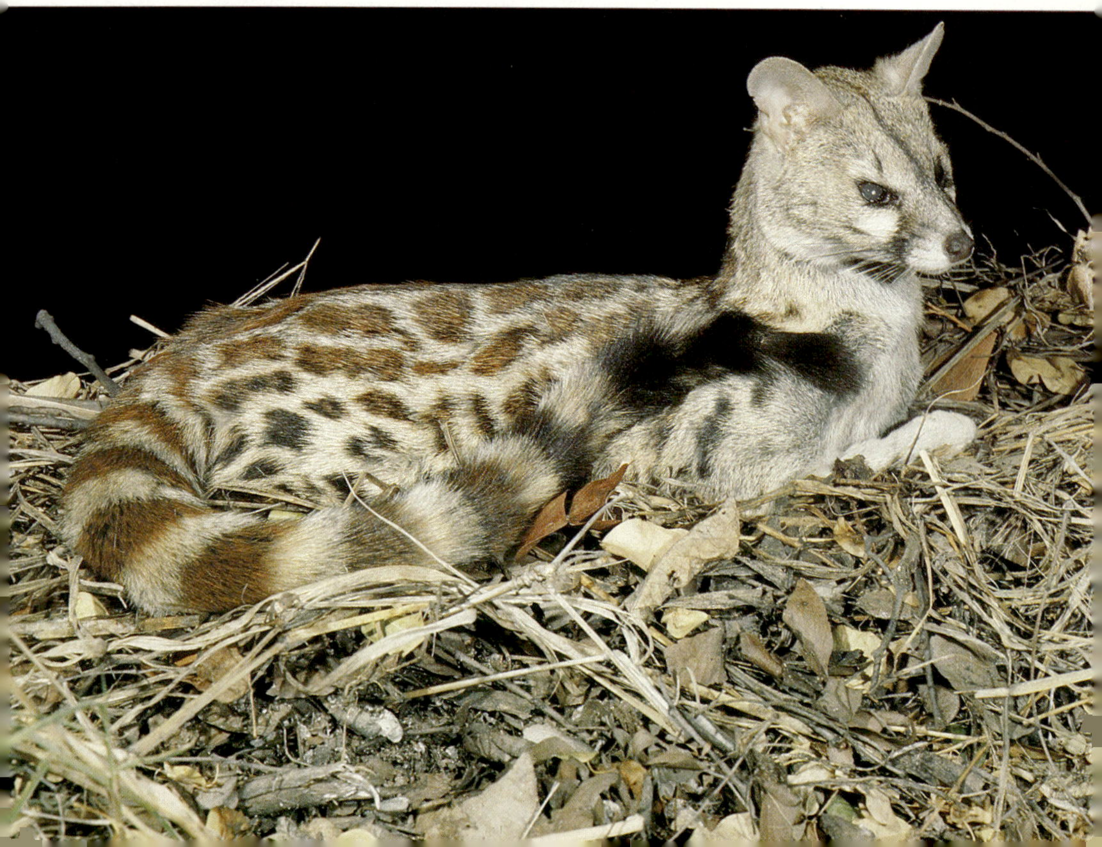

appear to be nomadic and have no fixed den or shelter but move around and stay in the vicinity of fruiting trees for as long as fruit is available. They have ventral and pregenital scent glands adapted to the arboreal existence, which are used for marking branches over which they move. Their call is similar to the mew of a cat.

BREEDING

The young are born in suitable lairs in trees and number two to three per litter.

ENEMIES AND DISEASE

Probably fall prey to large raptors such as the crowned eagle and large predators such as leopards.

Previous page: Strong toes and a long tail aid the palm civet in its largely arboreal existence.

Opposite
Top: The small-spotted genet has dark legs and a crest of hair along its back.

Below: The large, reddish-brown blotches and lack of a dorsal hair crest are characteristics of the rusty-spotted genet.

SMALL-SPOTTED GENET
Genetta genetta Linnaeus, 1758

A: Kleinkolmuskejaatkat

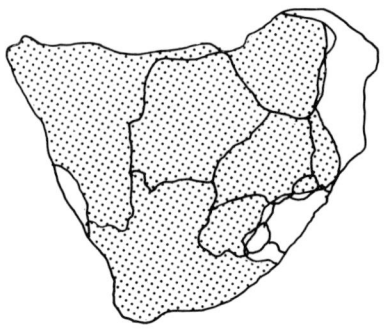

DESCRIPTION

Both genets have long bodies and tails, short legs and relatively large ears. The small-spotted has dark brown to black spots on a pale white background. The spots run in lines laterally down the body to the bushy tail, which has dark rings around it and ends in a white tip. Unlike the rusty-spotted, it has a crest of dark hair running down the length of the back. The face is delicately marked with white patches under the eyes and black between the nose and eyes. The legs are dark as opposed to the usually pale-coloured legs of the next species. Males have a mass of up to 2,4 kg and females 2,0 kg. Head and body measurements are 47–56 cm, and the tail is 41–44 cm long.

DISTRIBUTION AND HABITAT

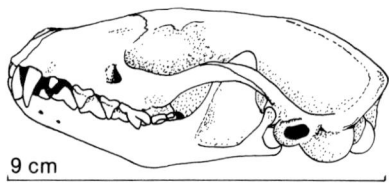

9 cm

Widespread throughout most of the region but appears to be absent from most of Natal. In Mozambique they occur only in the south. They have a wide habitat tolerance but are associated with woodland, ravines, large trees and/or rocky areas.

FEEDING BEHAVIOUR

These carnivores actively hunt a variety of insects such as beetles, termites and grass-hoppers, other invertebrates including scorpions and sun spiders and also small rodents, frogs, lizards, snakes and birds. They will readily take poultry. A variety of wild fruit and cultivated fruit such as grapes and figs also feature in their diet. They have small, retractile claws, similar to those of cats, which are readily used when climbing trees. They also forage a great deal on the ground. The ears are used to locate potential prey.

Actual Size

HABITS

The small-spotted genet is largely nocturnal and solitary, hiding in rock crevices, hollow tree trunks, a dense bush or similar refuge during the day. When cornered they will spit and growl much like a domestic cat. They depend on their climbing ability to escape predators such as dogs. These animals deposit their dung in middens in various situations. In the Matopos (Zimbabwe) old grain bins are often used. Other sites include old raptor nests, bare rock, old drinking troughs and prominent logs. They are sometimes mobbed by birds during the day when lying in a tree or bush.

BREEDING

Two to four young are born after a gestation period of about 70 days. A suitable refuge such as a rock crevice or hollow log is used. Breeding takes place during the summer months from October to February. The young are born with a slight covering of hair which shows the adult colour pattern. Their eyes are closed at birth and they can mew quietly.

ENEMIES AND DISEASE

A number are destroyed annually because of their habit of raiding poultry and some fall victim to problem animal control exercises. The major natural enemies of this species are the large birds of prey such as martial eagle, crowned eagle and Cape eagle owl. Larger predators such as the leopard also catch and eat genets. These animals have been known to contract rabies, but little else is known about diseases which affect them.

RUSTY-SPOTTED GENET
Genetta tigrina (Schreber, 1776)

E: Large-spotted genet
A: Rooikolmuskejaatkat, grootkolmuskejaatkat

DESCRIPTION

This description must be read in conjunction
with that of the previous species. The main
differences between the two are the larger
and more rusty-coloured spots of this
species, the usually pale legs and absence of
a crest of hair along the back. The body hair
is also shorter and the large spots vary a
great deal in colour. The tail lacks the white
tip. The rusty-spotted is also slightly
smaller, with a body mass of 1,0 kg to
2,2 kg. Head and body measure 42–58 cm
and the tail 38–45 cm.

DISTRIBUTION AND HABITAT

The range of the rusty-spotted genet
overlaps with the previous species in some
areas, but it has a more limited distribution.
It occurs in northern Botswana and the
Caprivi, Zimbabwe, Mozambique, the
eastern half of the Transvaal, Swaziland,
Natal and along the eastern coastal areas to
Cape Town. This species seems to be more
closely associated with well-watered areas
and woodland. They are common in rocky
terrain with well-wooded ravines.

FEEDING BEHAVIOUR

The diet of this animal is much the same as
that of the previous species but appears to
concentrate on small rodents. They also
feed on moles, bats, lizards, snakes,
geckos, various birds and their eggs, frogs,
insects such as termites, grasshoppers,
beetles, crickets, caterpillars and moths,
other invertebrates including sun spiders,
scorpions and centipedes, and vegetable
matter such as various wild fruits, avocado
pear, grass and sugar cane. They have also
been recorded feeding on baby crocodiles at
a breeding station and will play havoc with
poultry. Although they can climb very well,

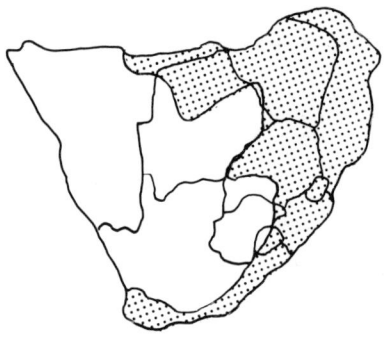

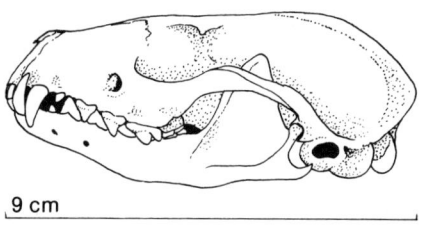

9 cm

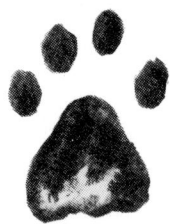

Actual Size

most of their foraging takes place on the
ground and the ears play an important part
in finding prey. They will also scavenge to
some degree and become quite tame around
camp fires in certain protected areas, where
they pick up scraps lying around on the
ground.

HABITS

Similar in habits to the previous species. They are also nocturnal and solitary, spending much of the daylight hours sleeping in rock crevices, hollow trees, dense bushes or even in old raptor nests. When cornered they will spit and growl like cats, and very small ones make a mewing sound. They also use dung middens in much the same way, located in similar situations.

BREEDING

Two to five young are born during the summer months in a suitable site such as a hollow tree or rock crevice. They leave the den when about two to three months old to explore the surrounding areas. The gestation period is about 60–70 days and the female cares for the young.

ENEMIES AND DISEASE

As with the previous species a small number are destroyed by man. Their main enemies are the birds of prey and large carnivores. They have also been known to contract rabies.

WHITE-TAILED MONGOOSE
Ichneumia albicauda G. Cuvier, 1829

A: Groot witstertmuishond, witstert-muishond

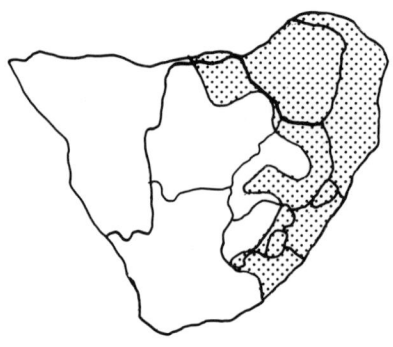

DESCRIPTION

A large and rather shaggy-looking mongoose with a body mass of up to 5 kg. The legs are black and the overall body colour is grey tinged with dark brown, the tail is long-haired, bushy and mostly white. Some individuals have quite dark tails, and very dark body colouration. Head and body measurements are 50–80 cm, tail 37–45 cm, and shoulder height 25 cm.

DISTRIBUTION AND HABITAT

This species is found in the north-eastern sector of the region which includes northern Botswana, Zimbabwe, Mozambique, northern and eastern Transvaal, Swaziland, Natal and Transkei. It is a species of the better-watered savanna areas.

FEEDING BEHAVIOUR

These animals feed mainly on insects and their larvae and are often found around old cattle kraals, probably searching for dung-beetle larvae. They forage by using their nose and eyes, and dig with the claws of the front feet. They also feed on small rodents and insectivores, carrion, birds, various reptiles, frogs and invertebrates such as crabs, earthworms and centipedes.

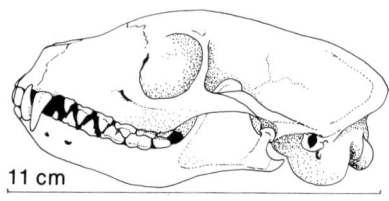

11 cm

HABITS

They are nocturnal and generally solitary, but are sometimes seen in pairs or a family group consisting of a mother with young. When alarmed they will arch the back, raise the tail and erect the long hairs along the back and tail, which has the effect of making the animal look twice its normal size. When on the move they scurry along with the head held lower than the rest of the body. They may growl or give a sharp bark when alarmed. They are rarely seen because they are nocturnal and inhabit rather dense bush.

Actual Size

BREEDING

Little is recorded about this animal, but they are said to have two to three young during the summer months. A dead female was found to have six foetuses.

ENEMIES AND DISEASE

Little is recorded, but they probably fall prey to large predators such as the leopard, and would also be taken by large birds of prey if the opportunity arose.

MELLER'S MONGOOSE
Rhynchogale melleri (Gray, 1865)

A: Mellerse muishond

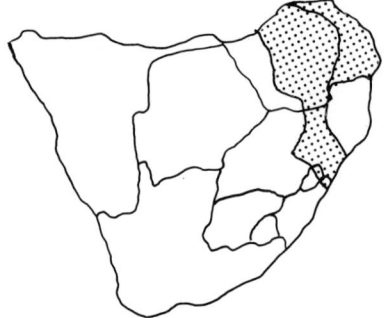

DESCRIPTION

A shaggy-coated mongoose, dark brown in colour, with black legs and a black tail. Smaller than the previous species. Very similar to the Selous' mongoose in size and shape. To confuse the issue, Meller's mongoose also comes in a grey form with dark legs and a white tip to the end of the tail, almost identical to the normal Selous' mongoose and very similar to a juvenile white-tailed mongoose. There are three major differences between the Meller's and other species, however: the Meller's has a thick upper lip without a naked groove running from nose to mouth, the cheek teeth are rounded and flattened on the occlusal (upper) surface and the fur on the side of the neck has an unusual parting, which forms a distinct crest. It has a body mass of about 2,5 kg, a head and body length of about 45 cm and a tail 30–40 cm long.

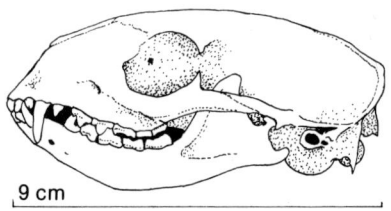

9 cm

DISTRIBUTION AND HABITAT

This mongoose is found in the eastern half of Zimbabwe, Mozambique and the eastern Transvaal lowveld. It is a species of the higher-rainfall areas of the region and is associated with tall grassland, savanna woodland and granite areas.

FEEDING BEHAVIOUR

They appear to feed fairly extensively on harvester termites, also other insects such as grasshoppers and beetles, small rodents,

Hind Foot

Actual Size

Opposite: The long-haired, bushy tail of the appropriately named white-tailed mongoose is a good field characteristic of this species.

Overleaf
Top: Meller's mongoose is recognised by its brown body, black bushy tail and a distinctive parting of hairs on its neck.

Below: When alarmed the water mongoose arches its back and erects its hair, thereby creating an illusion of greater size.

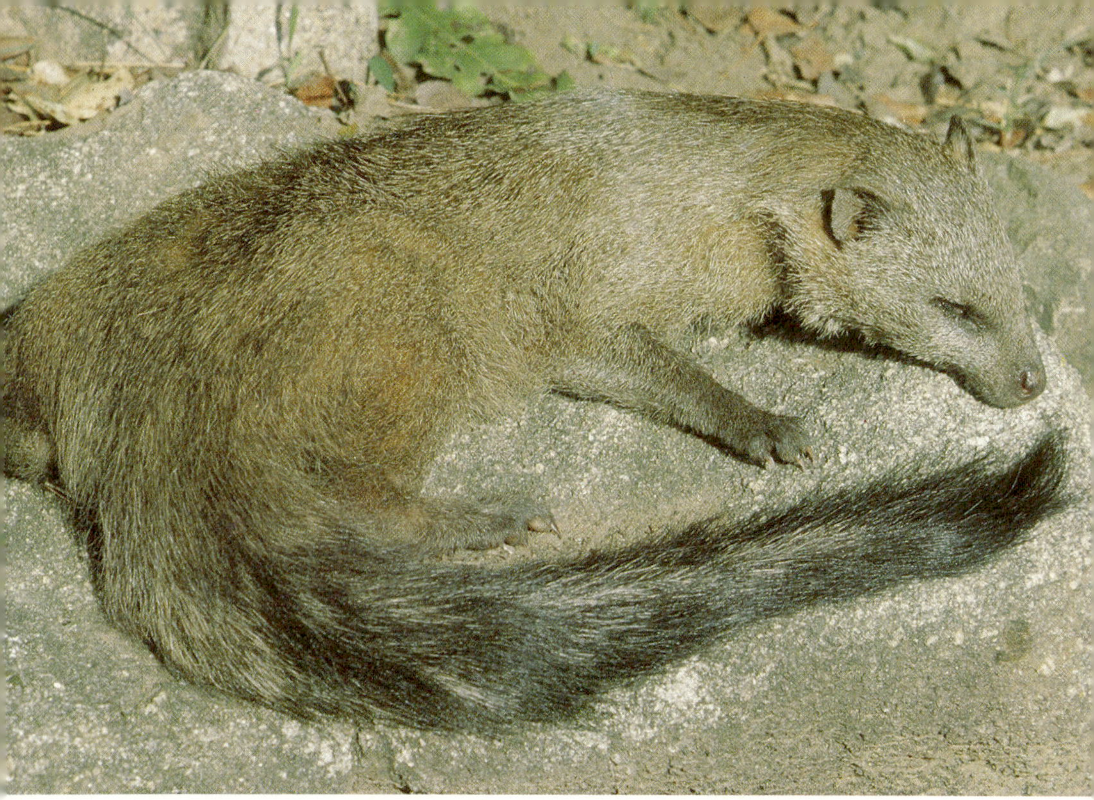

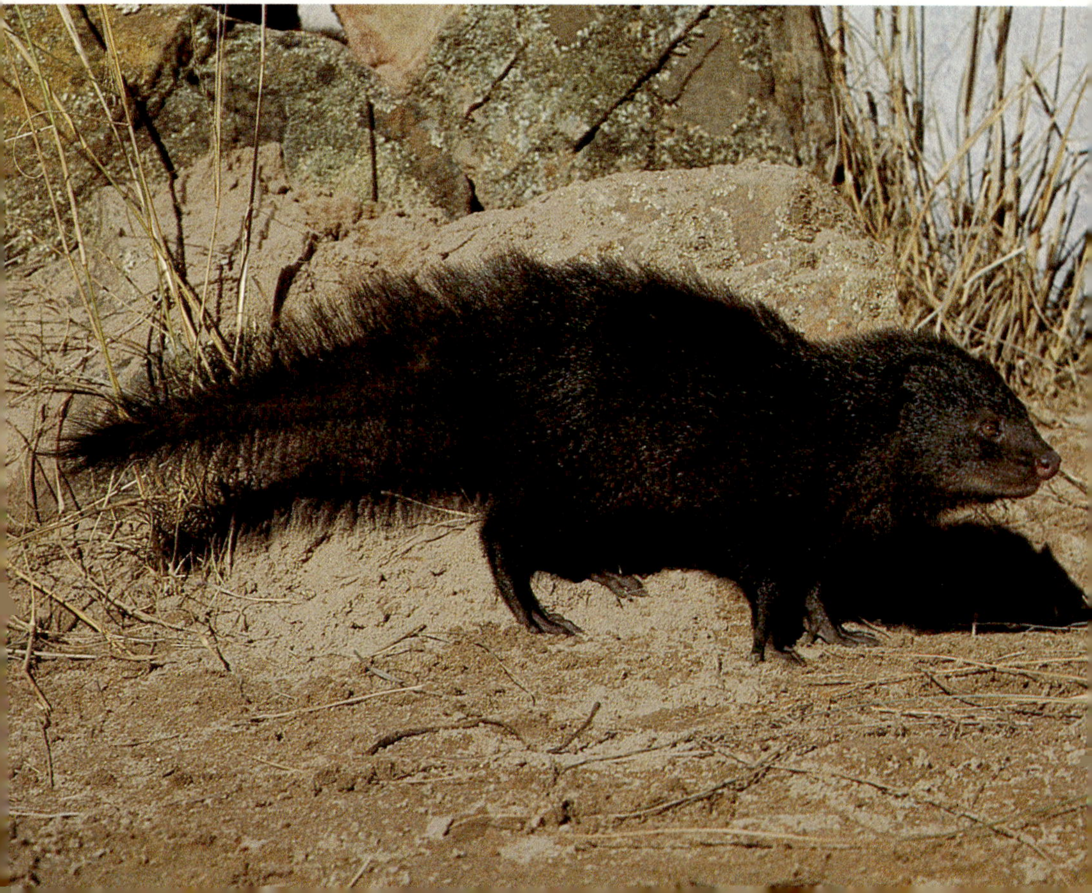

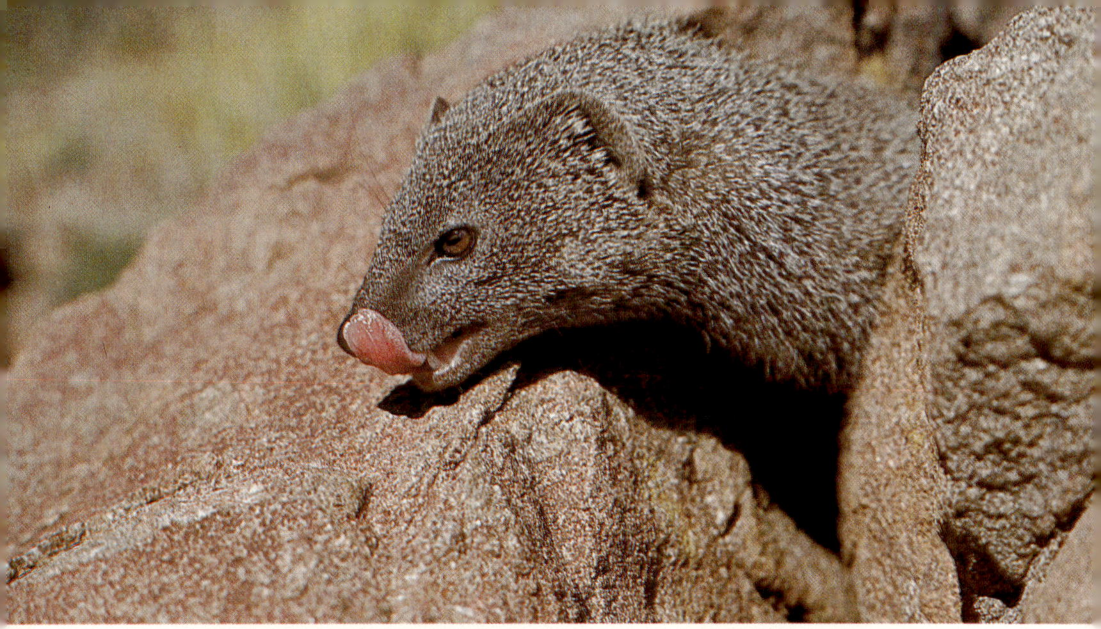

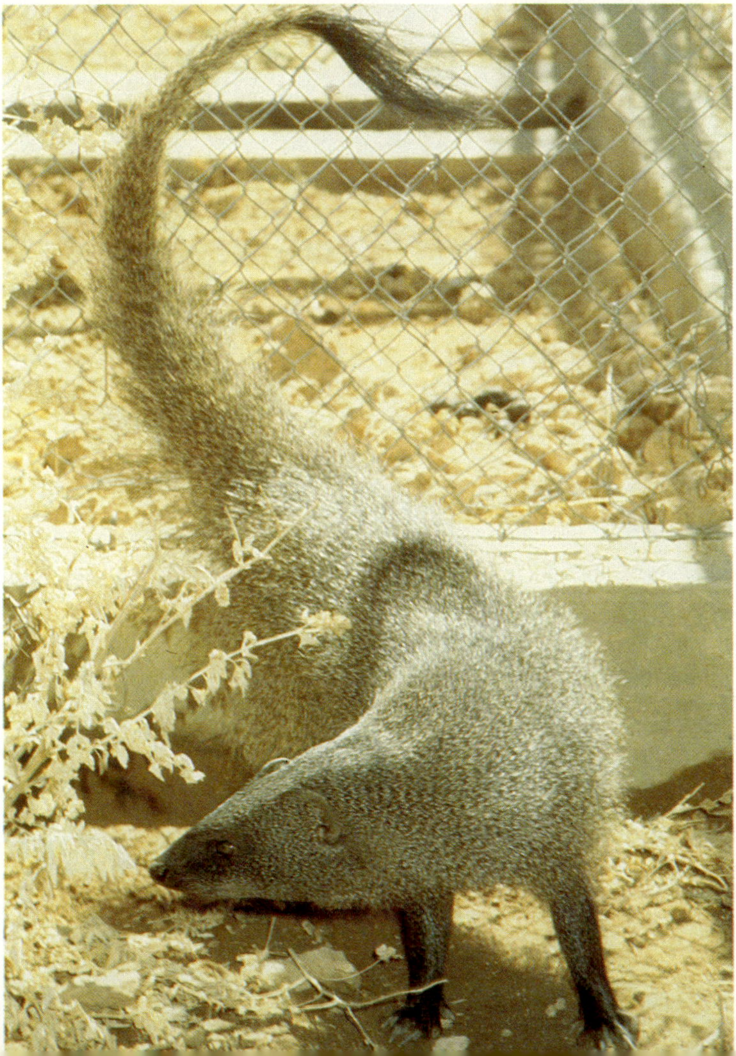

reptiles and fruit. They have been observed foraging in leaf litter at the base of a granite koppie, and feeding on termites on a lawn in the Matopos (Zimbabwe).

HABITS

Little is known about this elusive nocturnal species, but they appear to be solitary by nature.

BREEDING

Two to three young are produced during the summer months.

ENEMIES AND DISEASE

Little is recorded. They probably fall prey to large predators such as leopard, and birds such as Cape eagle owl and large eagles on occasion.

Previous page
Top: The Cape grey mongoose often takes refuge in rock crevices.

Below: A tapering tail and dark face are two distinctive features of the large grey mongoose.

Opposite
The smallest of the mongooses is the dark-brown-coloured dwarf mongoose, which is a very social creature.
Top inset: Dwarf mongooses often live in termite mounds.

WATER MONGOOSE
Atilax paludinosus G. Cuvier, 1829

E: Marsh mongoose. *A:* Watermuishond, kommetjiesgatmuishond

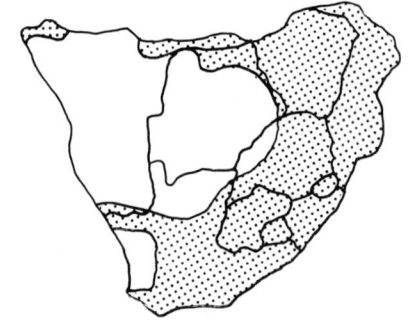

DESCRIPTION

A large dark brown, long-haired mongoose
with a shortish, thick tail which tapers
rapidly. The eyes are a conspicuous amber
colour and the nose pink to orange. It runs
with the head held low and the hindquarters
slightly raised. The body mass of adults may
be as much as 5,5 kg. This is a very distinct species and is not easily mistaken
for another mongoose. Head and body
measurements are 45–64 cm, with tail 30–
40 cm and a shoulder height of about 15 cm.

DISTRIBUTION AND HABITAT

The water mongoose has a patchy distribution although it appears to be widespread in
the eastern half of the region. This is because it is restricted to areas with permanent water, even though it will forage some
way away from a water source. Occurs in
northern Botswana, Zimbabwe, Mozambique, south through the Orange Free State
to Cape Town. Absent from the more arid
parts of the western Cape and SWA/
Namibia.

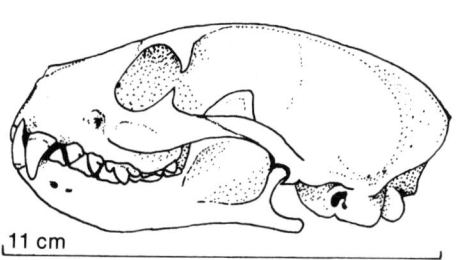

11 cm

FEEDING BEHAVIOUR

This mongoose spends much of its time in
shallow water in search of crabs, frogs and
aquatic insects which form the major part of
its diet. It has naked toes adapted to the
aquatic environment, for swimming and
walking in soft mud. It will also forage away
from water in search of other food, which
includes small rodents, insects, birds
(including ducks and domestic poultry),
lizards, snakes and invertebrates. It also
feeds on carrion, fish and freshwater
mussels which are broken open by flicking
them through the hind legs onto a hard
object such as a rock. Other items may be
broken in a similar fashion. It is reputed to
raid the nests of crocodiles.

Actual Size

HABITS

This is an elusive nocturnal species which is
rarely seen because it inhabits riverine
areas where the visibility is poor. Usually
solitary and may on occasion be seen

foraging in the late afternoon. Its presence in an area is indicated by the spoor in wet mud, and by latrines or dung middens near the water's edge. This mongoose is a strong swimmer and takes readily to water when alarmed, swimming with the back and dorsal part of the tail sticking out of the water. When cornered it arches the back, erects the hair, utters short successive barks and emits a musky smell from the anal glands. It will also growl loudly through the nose. The anal glands are used in marking areas where the mongoose is active.

BREEDING

Two to three young are born in burrows, rock crevices or other suitable refuges near water.

ENEMIES AND DISEASE

May be killed by large predators such as the leopard and there is a record of this species being taken by a honey badger. Large birds of prey also take the water mongoose. Occasionally becomes infected with rabies. Sometimes killed as poultry thieves.

LARGE GREY MONGOOSE

Herpestes ichneumon (Linnaeus, 1758)

E: Egyptian mongoose, Cape ichneumon. *A:* Groot grysmuishond

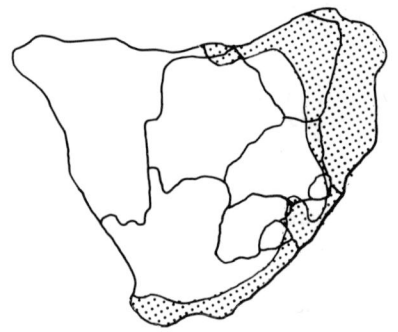

DESCRIPTION

A large grey mongoose (as the name implies) with a speckled coat caused by bands of colour on the individual hairs. The legs of this animal are dark brown to black and the tail tapers from a bushy base to a thin black tip. It attains a body mass of 3,6 kg which is somewhat lighter than the previous species. A relatively long animal, with head and body measurements of 50–60 cm, and a tail 30–55 cm long.

DISTRIBUTION AND HABITAT

Found along the coastal belt from Cape Town to Zululand, eastern Transvaal lowveld, eastern and northern Zimbabwe, northern Botswana, eastern Caprivi and most of Mozambique. This animal inhabits the humid to sub-humid areas of grassland and savanna woodland and coastal fynbos in the Cape. An animal of dense vegetation, it is thus rarely seen despite being largely diurnal.

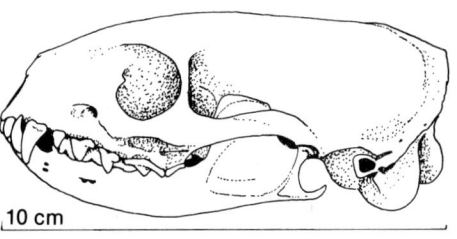

10 cm

FEEDING BEHAVIOUR

The diet consists largely of small rodents such as the vleirat, birds, frogs, toads, reptiles, fish, earthworms, insects and other invertebrates, and fruit including avocado pear.

HABITS

These animals may be quite active during daylight hours. They are usually solitary, but may sometimes be seen in pairs. They can swim well and are quite often associated with moist areas.

BREEDING

Two to four young are born in a burrow, hollow tree or similar refuge.

Actual Size

ENEMIES AND DISEASE

Nothing recorded, but probably taken by large predators and birds of prey on occasion. May contract rabies.

CAPE GREY MONGOOSE

Galerella pulverulentus (Wagner, 1839)

A: Kleingrysmuishond, Kaapse grysmuishond

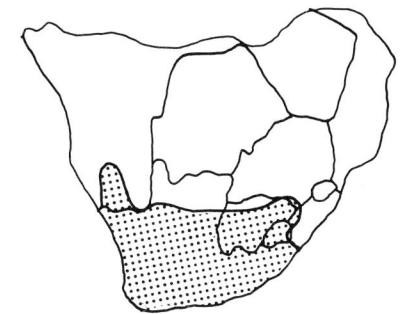

DESCRIPTION

This is a dark grey to pale grey mongoose, similar to the slender mongoose but more robust and with longer hair. Has been mistaken for the slender mongoose in northern SWA/Namibia, but latest information indicates little overlap between these two species. The body colour is a definite grey, speckled with white from the colour banding on the hairs, with paler underparts and slightly darker legs. Males have a mass of around 825 g and females just over 700 g. Head and body length is 27–46 cm and tail length 20–34 cm.

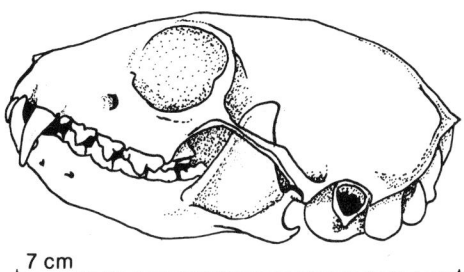

7 cm

DISTRIBUTION AND HABITAT

This animal is endemic to the southern parts of the region; in South Africa, south of the Orange and Vaal rivers and western Natal. Also occurs in southern SWA/Namibia, Lesotho and Transkei. It may be found in a wide range of habitats but is more common in dense thickets and rocky terrain. Ranges from the coastal areas through to the arid Karoo, and is a generally abundant species where it occurs.

Actual Size

FEEDING BEHAVIOUR

This small mongoose feeds on a great variety of food and is very partial to carrion of most kinds, including carcasses as large as eland. Often found scavenging around human habitation and on road kills. Apart from carrion it feeds on small rodents, birds and their eggs, insects and other invertebrates and wild fruit, and may even raid beehives. Reptiles and amphibians are also included in its diet.

HABITS

This is a solitary, diurnal species and is usually encountered dashing across a road. It forages actively in thickets and rocky areas and is sometimes mobbed by birds. It takes refuge in old holes in banks, old buildings, rock crevices, hollow logs, old pipes and dense thickets. This species may sometimes be seen sunning itself near a refuge but is quick to react to danger. It does not use dung middens and in captivity will mark its area with secretions from the anal glands. When cornered it growls and does not hesitate to bite. Often uses foot paths to move through an area.

BREEDING

One to three young are born in the spring and summer months in a shallow crevice or refuge as described above. A newborn litter of two was found among lucerne bales in a barn near Cradock late in August. At birth the youngsters have a sparse covering of grey hair, closed eyes, small sharp teeth and they utter soft grunts when hungry. Most of the suckling appears to take place on the two posterior nipples.

ENEMIES AND DISEASE

In the Mountain Zebra National Park near Cradock (South Africa) an adult was found in the stomach of a large Cape cobra. They also fall prey to large raptors including the crowned eagle, martial eagle, tawny eagle, and predators such as caracal and black-backed jackal, and would be killed by larger carnivores if they made contact with them. Many are killed in problem animal control exercises because of their scavenging, and a number are killed on the roads annually. May contract rabies.

SLENDER MONGOOSE
Galerella sanguinea (Rüppell, 1836)

A: Roooimuishond, swartkwasmuishond

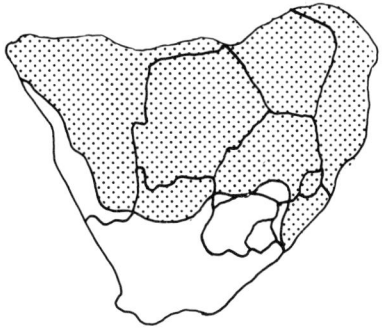

DESCRIPTION

As the name implies, this is a slender animal. The body colour varies greatly from a speckled yellow-brown to a speckled red-brown, the latter colour pattern being particularly characteristic in the north-western part of their range; the speckling is caused by black bands on the hair. A characteristic feature is the curved tail with a distinct black tip. It has amber eyes and a pink nose. (These notes must be compared with the previous species with which it could be confused.) The males have a mass of up to 640 g and the females are slightly lighter with a mass of up to 530 g, head and body length 26–33 cm, tail about 25 cm long, shoulder height about 13 cm.

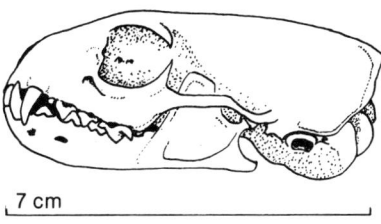

7 cm

DISTRIBUTION AND HABITAT

This mongoose is generally found north of the Orange and Vaal rivers. Its range includes SWA/Namibia, most of Botswana, the northern Cape and most of Natal below the Drakensberg, then stretches northward to include the rest of the region. It has a wide habitat tolerance but is common in open savanna country and has adapted to an urban environment, living in drain pipes and gardens.

FEEDING BEHAVIOUR

As with the previous species, they feed on a variety of food, but mainly on insects such as termites, beetles and grasshoppers, also birds and their eggs, rats, mice and invertebrates such as scorpions and sun spiders. Eggs are broken by flicking them through the hind legs with the front feet onto a hard object. These plucky little carnivores also feed on reptiles such as lizards and snakes, including cobras and young mambas. Unfortunately, they are also partial to poultry, and will take carrion.

Actual Size

HABITS

This is a diurnal, solitary species, although sometimes seen in pairs and often encountered in urban gardens and on roads. They become quite tame and will drink from garden ponds, also taking scraps of food left out. It is not advisable to encourage these animals because they are rabies carriers.

They can climb if necessary, but generally forage on the ground, often taking refuge in old termite mounds and rocky outcrops. They are often mobbed by birds when out foraging. When cornered they will spit and growl loudly. A common species where they occur.

BREEDING

One to four young are born in a termite mound, hollow tree, rock crevice or similar refuge, after a gestation period of about 45 days. The young are sometimes carried by the scruff of the neck to a new refuge, and when older will follow the mother in procession.

ENEMIES AND DISEASE

These animals are preyed on by a number of large birds such as the tawny eagle, martial eagle, African hawk eagle, Cape eagle owl and crowned eagle; also by large predators such as leopard. Many are killed annually in problem animal control exercises and a number are destroyed as poultry thieves. They may be a problem in some areas as a carrier of rabies because of their close association with man.

Opposite: The banded mongoose has a pink nose and characteristic dark bands on its back.

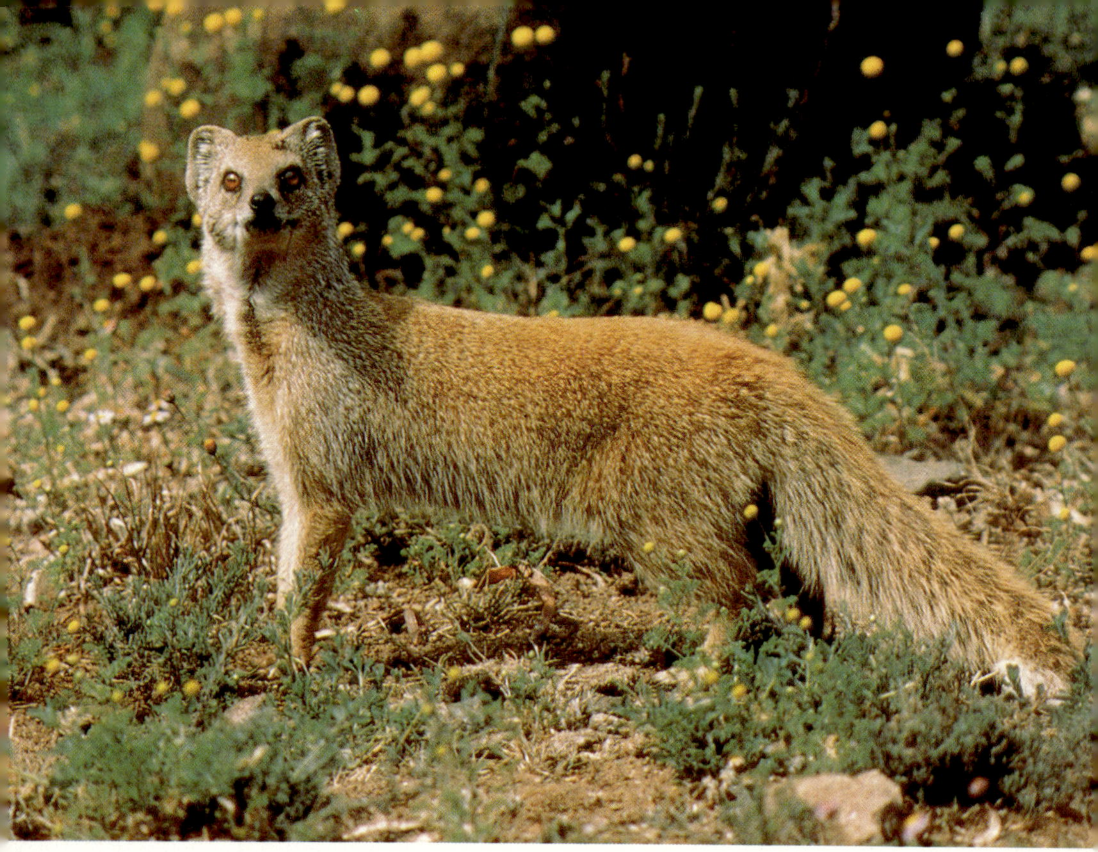

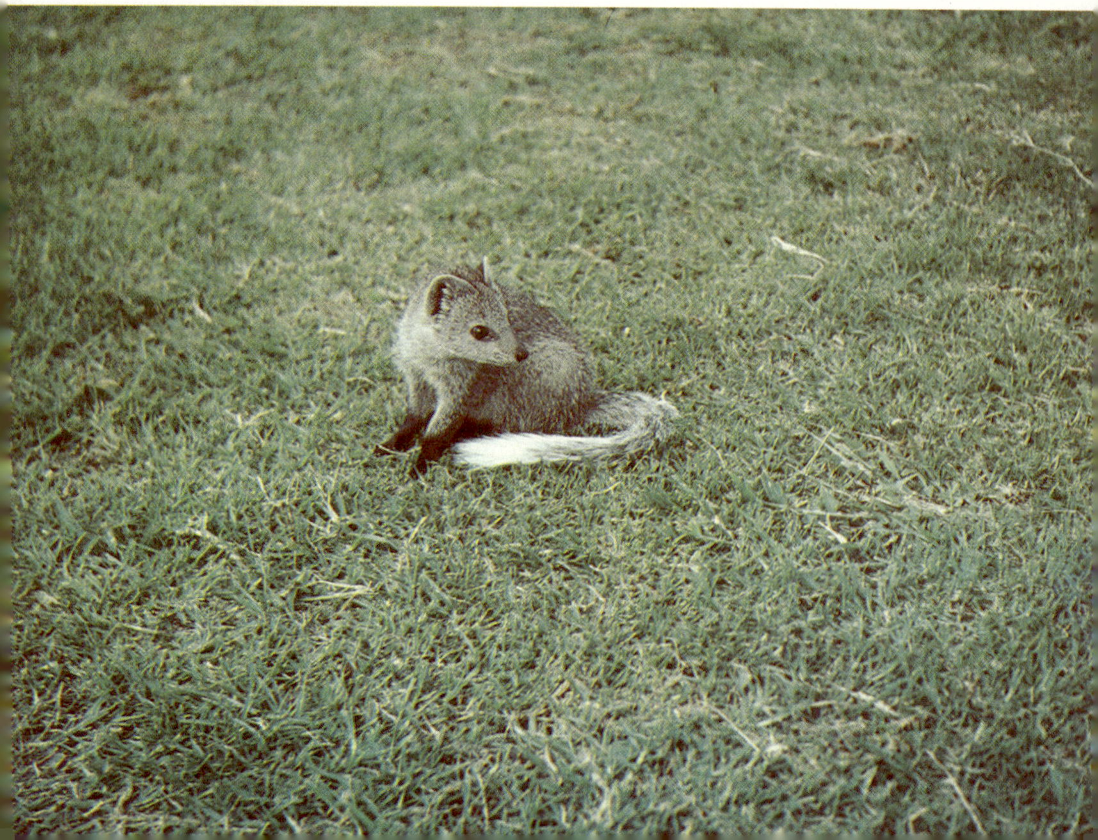

DWARF MONGOOSE
Helogale parvula Sundevall, 1846

A: Dwergmuishond

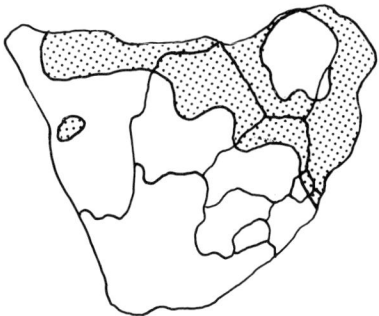

DESCRIPTION

This is the smallest carnivore in the region and cannot be mistaken. The body is a very dark brown, almost black at a distance, and the tail relatively short and pointed. It has sharp digging claws on the front feet and quite a compact build for a mongoose. The body mass in adults is about 350 g, head and body length 18–25 cm, tail 15–20 cm long, and shoulder height about 7 cm.

DISTRIBUTION AND HABITAT

Occurs in northern Botswana, SWA/ Namibia, western and south-western Zimbabwe, the northern and eastern parts of South Africa, Swaziland and over most of Mozambique. It is generally a species of the dry savanna areas in the region, often found in rocky broken country.

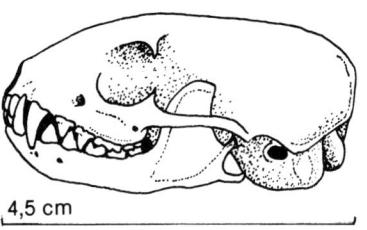

4,5 cm

FEEDING BEHAVIOUR

These little mongooses feed mainly on insects, especially beetles, but will take reptiles, small rodents and insectivores, and a variety of invertebrates such as sun spiders, scorpions, centipedes, worms and spiders and others unearthed while scratching around. Most of the foraging is done by searching through leaf litter and stony ground. Birds will be taken when the opportunity arises and eggs are broken in typical mongoose fashion, with a fast flick through the back legs.

Actual Size

HABITS

This is a gregarious species which moves about during daylight hours in groups of up to 15 or more individuals. They forage about noisily in leaf litter and under bushes, or in rubble, all the while making a chittering communication call. They also utter a sharp alarm call which will send the entire group scurrying away to the nearest cover. They are inquisitive little creatures and it does not

---

Opposite
Top: The yellow mongoose has a bushy tail with a characteristic pale tip.

Below: A juvenile Selous' mongoose has the typical white tail, black legs and pale grey coat of the adult.

take long for them to emerge from cover to see what the alarm was all about. They will also sit on their hind legs in an upright position to observe the surrounding area. They live in old logs, rock crevices, old termitaria, stone walls and old burrows in the ground. The dung is deposited in some quantities around the entrance to the refuge and is largely composed of finely ground insect remains. In Kenya a unique, mutually cooperative foraging and guarding system exists between dwarf mongooses on the one hand and the yellow-billed and Von der Decken's hornbills on the other. Parties of mongooses and hornbills move together, with the birds taking insects flushed out of the grass by the mongooses and in return giving warning to the mongooses of their predators.

BREEDING

Up to four young are born after a gestation period of 45–50 days in refuges as described above. Adults sometimes carry the young by the scruff of the neck.

ENEMIES AND DISEASE

They fall prey to a number of large raptors and could be taken by larger predators when encountered. They are also likely to contract rabies.

BANDED MONGOOSE
Mungos mungo Gmelin, 1788

A: Gebande muishond

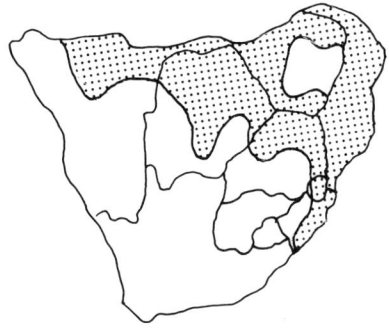

DESCRIPTION

This animal is grey in colour with darker legs and feet and very distinct dark bands across the lower back and rump. These bands are more distinct in older animals. It has a pink nose and dark eyes; a longish tail which is quite bushy at the base. The body mass is about 1,4 kg, head and body length 30–40 cm, tail length 15–25 cm, shoulder height about 13 cm.

DISTRIBUTION AND HABITAT

Their distribution and habitat is much the same as that of the previous species and they are found in the dry savanna regions of northern Botswana, northern SWA/Namibia, western and southern Zimbabwe, the northern and eastern parts of South Africa down to Natal, Swaziland and Mozambique.

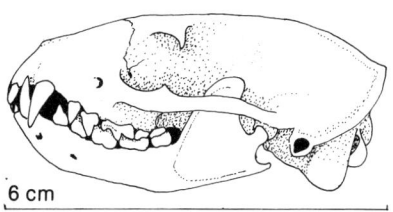

6 cm

FEEDING BEHAVIOUR

The diet of the banded mongoose consists largely of invertebrates such as beetles, grasshoppers, other insects, sun spiders, scorpions and centipedes, which are encountered in their foraging sprees. They work as a group, lifting stones, digging around in leaf litter, antelope dung heaps and other debris and generally inspecting every nook and cranny. The claws on the front feet are used for digging and scratching around. They also feed on reptiles, small mammals and birds. In captivity they will feed on all red meats presented to them and develop a taste for a variety of household groceries. Where they occur in coastal dune areas, they will feed on snails, the shells being broken by flicking them through the hind legs onto a hard object. Eggs are dealt with in a similar fashion and they have been recorded flicking stones at ostrich eggs in an attempt to break the shell.

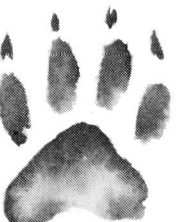

Actual Size

HABITS

This species is diurnal and very gregarious, occurring in groups of 30 or more. They are terrestrial and move about in these large groups, chittering away to each other as a means of comunication. They have a habit of periodically sitting up motionless on their haunches to survey the surrounding area and in this position resemble a series of small wooden stumps. Once the alarm is given they scurry away into the nearest shelter, but their more permanent refuges are old anthills, rocky crevices and piles of rubble on occasion. In captivity they have a habit of marking objects with their anal glands; they make very good entertaining pets but may deliver nasty bites to unwelcome guests. They growl, jerk spit, utter an alarm chirp and make a variety of other sounds.

BREEDING

As many as eight young have been recorded in a single litter. These are born during the summer months in a suitable refuge after a gestation period of about 60 days. Females are reputed to suckle more than one litter and this is probably part of the communal society they have evolved. Numerous young from the age of three weeks are often seen with groups of these animals. Small young are sometimes carried by the scruff of the neck when moving to a new den. Any member of the pack may transport the young and the male has an important role in looking after them.

ENEMIES AND DISEASE

This species is taken by many of the large raptors such as the martial eagle, tawny eagle and Cape eagle owl. They are also eaten by large predators such as the leopard. Despite their gregarious nature and occurrence along with jackals and other animals associated with rabies, this species is not suspected of rabies transmission. This does not, however, mean they will not contract the disease.

YELLOW MONGOOSE
Cynictis penicillata G. Cuvier, 1829

E: Red mongoose. A: Geelmeerkat, rooimeerkat

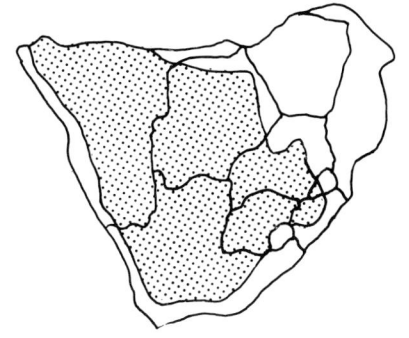

DESCRIPTION

This species is a distinct yellow colour with conspicuous white to pale yellow tail tip. The tail is quite bushy, especially at the base. The ears are relatively large for a mongoose, running vertically down the side of the head and protruding slightly above the pointed face when viewed from the front. The underparts are pale buff and the eyes orange-brown. Males are slightly more robust and larger than females and have a body mass of up to 1100 g. Females have a mass of about 1000 g. Head and body measurements are 30–40 cm and the tail is 20–25 cm long.

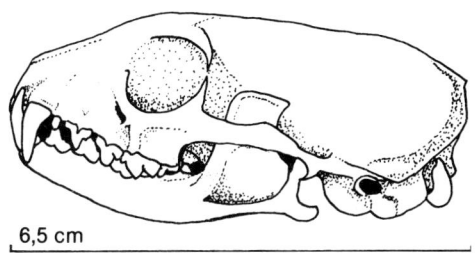

6,5 cm

DISTRIBUTION AND HABITAT

This animal has a wide distribution in the more arid areas of the region, occurring over most of the Cape Province, Orange Free State, Botswana, Lesotho and northern SWA/Namibia. It is absent from the coastal areas in general, and occurs marginally in north-western Zimbabwe. This is a species of the more open short grassland, dwarf shrub and arid areas; it occupies much the same habitat as the suricate.

Actual Size

FEEDING BEHAVIOUR

This species is a fairly selective feeder with a diet that consists almost entirely of insects, termites, beetles and grasshoppers accounting for 80 per cent of its diet. It is, therefore, a useful animal to the farmer. They also feed on carrion, frogs, small mammals, birds, reptiles and invertebrates such as centipedes and sun spiders. Fruit is also taken, as well as ground-nuts, beans, maize, grass seeds, sunflower seeds and various berries. The long canines of this species are probably more closely related to social behaviour than feeding. They forage by working through an area, sniffing under possible prey refuges and digging with the claws on the front feet.

HABITS

These mongooses are diurnal and although generally solitary, they may be seen in pairs and live in packs of up to seven individuals at colonies. They live in a complicated series of burrows, often old springhare holes, which are excavated to their own needs with several chambers and a number of entrances. Much of their time is spent in and about these burrows which may be co-habited by other species including suricates, ground squirrels, and even animals such as cobras and bullfrogs. They are often seen lying near the burrows, sunning themselves in the morning, but forage away from these on their own. While away from the burrow and in the open, they have the habit of standing up on their hind legs to survey the surroundings. They have been observed feeding on termites in the middle of a flock of crowned guineafowl, neither feeding species showing any interest in the other. Several burrow systems may be used by a particular group of yellow mongoose, usually within a hundred metres of each other. They also have the habit, as with the dwarf mongoose, of leaving dung deposits at the entrance to burrows and have in addition several latrines away from the burrow system. The sex ratio of a group varies greatly and appears to be quite dynamic. They are relatively silent animals and little is known about the sounds they make.

BREEDING

From one to five young are born in a burrow and they remain quite attached to the den for some months, being quick to return to its safety when alarmed. The young are born during the summer months corresponding with a peak at the time of maximum rainfall.

ENEMIES AND DISEASE

The yellow mongoose falls prey to large raptors such as the martial and tawny eagles, also to large predators like leopard, caracal and hyaena. They are very prone to rabies and more than 90 per cent of confirmed cases in South Africa from wild carnivores are from this species. As a result some numbers are killed in control exercises.

SELOUS' MONGOOSE
Paracynictis selousi (de Winton, 1896)

A: Kleinwitstertmuishond

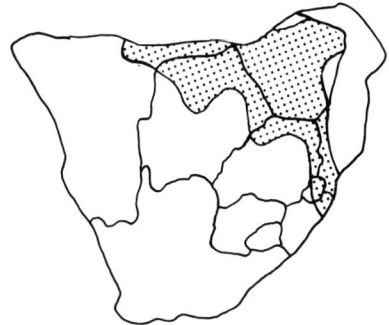

DESCRIPTION

This is a medium-sized, pale grey mongoose with dark legs, fairly large ears and a white tail. It is smaller than the white-tailed mongoose and has a body mass of about 2,5 kg when adult. It may also be confused with a colour phase of the Meller's mongoose and the description of this latter species should be referred to. Head and body measurements are about 45 cm, the tail about 30 cm long, and shoulder height about 20 cm.

DISTRIBUTION AND HABITAT

This species is generally absent from most parts of South Africa but does occur in northern and eastern Transvaal and northern Natal. It is quite widespread in Zimbabwe and northern Botswana and along the Kavango River in northern SWA/Namibia, but appears to be absent from most of Mozambique. It is a savanna species, generally associated with grassland areas, woodland and also hilly country.

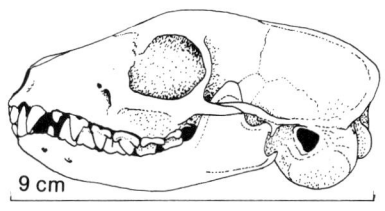

9 cm

FEEDING BEHAVIOUR

This species feeds mainly on insects, especially termites and beetles, but will also take small mammals, birds, reptiles and invertebrates such as sun spiders and scorpions. The claws on the front feet are effectively used for scratching around in leaf litter in search of food. It is reputed to eat small crocodiles.

Actual Size

HABITS

These animals are nocturnal and solitary by nature although family groups consisting of a female with young may be encountered. They live in a burrow system excavated by themselves, which has several entrances. They are fairly common in some areas but are usually encountered only at night and thus rarely seen by most people. When

caught the young will utter a screeching distress call.

BREEDING

Up to three young are born in burrows during the summer months.

ENEMIES AND DISEASE

They may be killed by large birds of prey and larger predators. One was found to have been killed by leopard and left on a road. A small number of road kills have been observed. They are likely to contract diseases such as rabies.

SURICATE
Suricata suricatta (Erxleben, 1777)

E: Meerkat. *A:* Stokstertmeerkat, graatjiemeerkat

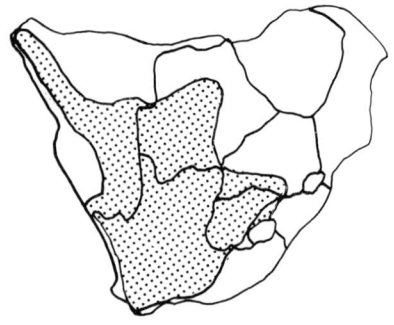

DESCRIPTION

This is a rather peculiar-looking little mongoose with a comical face. The body colour is generally a pale grey to almost white, with a reddish tinge to the hairs on the rump. The lower part of the back is covered with dark brown bars, while the tail is thin, rather stiff looking and black at the tip. The ear is not well defined and the pointed face is naked, with dark colouration around the large almost binocular eyes. It attains a body mass of up to 970 g, head and body length of 26–31 cm and tail length of 18–22 cm.

DISTRIBUTION AND HABITAT

This animal is quite widespread over the more arid and open areas of the region, in short grassland and dwarf shrub communities. It occurs widely in the Cape, Orange Free State, Lesotho, south-western Transvaal, southern Botswana and central SWA/Namibia.

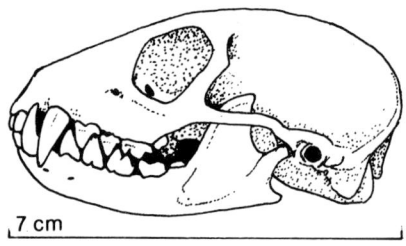

7 cm

FEEDING BEHAVIOUR

Although more than 80 per cent of their diet consists of insects, they feed on a wide variety of foodstuff. The insects taken are predominantly beetles, especially from the Scarabaeidae group, and the larvae and pupae of the Lepidoptera (moths and butterflies). They forage as a group and actively dig with the claws on the front feet when in search of food. Their diet also includes other insects, scorpions, spiders, maggots, centipedes, frogs, reptiles, small mammals, birds and vegetable matter such as fruit, small tubers, grass roots and the leaves of some succulents. Although they occupy the same habitat as the yellow mon-

Actual Size

Opposite: The suricate has a thin, black-tipped tail, brown bars on the back and a comical face. It moves around in packs during the day.

goose, they are less selective in their food requirements and co-exist without much competition.

HABITS

This mongoose is diurnal and very gregarious, occurring in packs of up to 40 individuals. The pack forages over a large area, systematically working the ground before returning to the burrow system where much of their time is spent. The zone around the burrow entrance is well used by animals lying in the sun grooming themselves or, particularly in the case of the young, as a play area. Although they will cohabit a burrow system with a variety of other animals such as the yellow mongoose, ground squirrel and even snakes, amphibians and certain birds, they pay little attention to the other species. A common and characteristic habit of the species is to stand upright on its hind legs, often on a vantage point such as a termite mound, rock, or log, to survey the surrounding area. They will sometimes sit relaxed on their haunches, sunning their underparts and quietly nodding off to sleep. When danger, such as a bird of prey, is sighted, they utter a loud 'waauk-waauk' which sends all members of the group scurrying away into the burrows or nearest cover. They also bark and will defend themselves vigorously when attacked. The composition of a pack varies greatly but there are generally as many males as there are females. Although they make good pets, they should be avoided because of their association with rabies.

BREEDING

As many as five young are born per litter in the self-excavated burrows where they live, after a gestation period of 60 to 70 days. The young are born with closed eyes, which open at about two weeks, and are sparsely covered with hair. They venture away from the burrow when about a month old and food is brought to them by the mother.

ENEMIES AND DISEASE

These animals often fall prey to large raptors such as the martial and tawny eagles and are probably taken by large carnivores on occasion. They contract rabies and should be avoided in areas where the disease is enzootic. Quite a number are killed by vehicles on main roads and others are exterminated in problem animal control exercises.

Opposite: A slender mongoose with the fawn colouring typical of this species over most of its range.

BUSHY-TAILED MONGOOSE
Bdeogale crassicauda Peters, 1852

A: Dikstertmuishond, borselstertmuishond

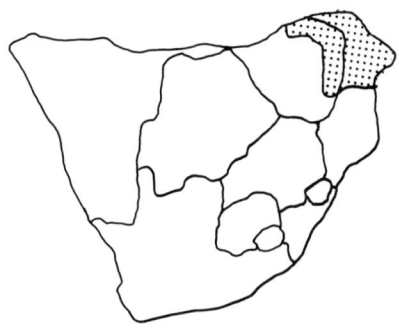

DESCRIPTION

This rare animal has dark, long coarse hair, giving it a shaggy appearance, with paler underparts and a bushy, almost black tail. The legs are also darker and the body is generally slender. It has a body mass of up to 2,5 kg, head and body length of 40–50 cm with a 20–30 cm long tail.
(Not illustrated)

DISTRIBUTION AND HABITAT

Occurs in north-eastern and eastern Zimbabwe and adjacent Mozambique, where it inhabits tall grassland and woodland areas. Also said to inhabit rocky terrain. Little else is known about its habitat requirements.

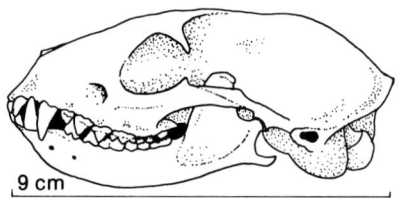

9 cm

FEEDING BEHAVIOUR

This animal appears to feed mainly on lizards and snakes of various kinds and will also feed on insects such as termites, beetles and grasshoppers, other invertebrates including slugs, small rodents and amphibians (frogs and toads). It has been suggested that it will feed on aquatic animals such as crabs.

HABITS

Of all the region's carnivores, the least known is the bushy-tailed mongoose. Most sightings of this species have been of solitary individuals out foraging at night. It is said to take refuge in rock crevices and hollow logs, but little information is available.

Hind Foot

Actual Size

HYAENAS AND AARDWOLF   FAMILY HYAENIDAE

These are large dog-like carnivores, which are in fact more closely related to the cats and civets. They have sloping backs, coarse hair, large front feet and small hind feet. There are four toes on each foot. The jaws of the hyaenas are powerful and the cheek teeth large. The aardwolf has weak dentition which is highly specialised for feeding on termites. The sense of smell is well developed. In hyaenas this aids the finding of carrion which forms a large part of their diet. The hyaenas and aardwolf share a unique form of scent marking: they paste a viscous secretion from anal glands on to grass stalks. The family is represented by three species in the region, the spotted and the brown hyaena of the subfamily Hyaeninae and the aardwolf of the subfamily Protelinae.

SPOTTED HYAENA
Crocuta crocuta (Erxleben, 1777)

A: Gevlekte hiëna

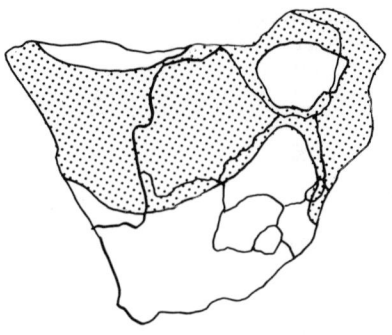

DESCRIPTION

The high shoulders, sloping back and hindquarters, a shuffling or loping gait and the large head swinging from side to side are characteristics of the spotted hyaena. It has relatively long, coarse fur, which is a khaki or buff colour varying to dull iron grey and almost black with variable dark spotting. The feet and muzzle are generally black as is the coarse brush of the short tail. The ears are rounded, the eyes large and the nostrils a curious tear-drop shape. There is a short bristly mane on the neck and shoulders which thins out with age. Spotted hyaenas stand 70–90 cm at the shoulder, their head and body measurements are about 95–150 cm, and tail about 30–36 cm. They weigh 50–85 kg. Females are generally larger and heavier than males. The sexes are not easily distinguished in the field as the external genitalia of the female superficially resemble those of the male, thus giving rise to the popular myth of hyaena hermaphroditism.

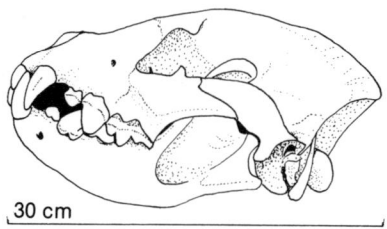

30 cm

DISTRIBUTION AND HABITAT

Spotted hyaenas have been exterminated throughout virtually all settled and stock-raising areas in Southern Africa. They are still common in the northern parts of Botswana, the southern Kalahari, much of the lower lying country of Zimbabwe and large parts of southern Mozambique. In South Africa they are confined to the Zululand game reserves, the Kalahari Gemsbok National Park, the Kruger Park and adjoining areas and the Limpopo Valley. In SWA/Namibia they are found scattered in the farming areas, in parts of the Namib, Etosha and are more widespread in the north-eastern regions. Spotted hyaena occupy a wide range of habitats from desert, through arid shrublands, savannas, woodland and even evergreen forests in Hluhluwe. They are generally more

4/5 Actual Size
Forefoot

abundant in open savanna country such as the central region of the Kruger Park with large populations of plains game.

FEEDING BEHAVIOUR

Long regarded as being a cowardly scavenger, the spotted hyaena is in fact a formidable hunter, possessing an acute sense of smell, keen eyesight, and a high degree of social cooperation. Packs of hyaenas pull down animals as large as wildebeest and zebra, especially injured or sick animals. Spotted hyaenas are most accurately described as opportunistic hunters and scavengers. Apart from killing their own prey, hyaenas will readily take the remains of the kills of other predators, or any dead animals they may come across during their nocturnal foraging. They have a digestive system which is highly efficient and can cope with a diverse range of material including meat, skin, bones and offal. They even eat the faeces of other carnivores from which they can extract nourishment. In the Kruger National Park spotted hyaenas generally forage singly or in small groups of two or three animals, and this is probably because of the generally dense vegetation; the scattered individuals thus cover a larger area more effectively. The prey taken varies with the season and consists mainly of impala, young wildebeest and zebra foals. During the impala-lambing season the hyaena may live almost exclusively on impala lambs. Spotted hyaenas have been recorded feeding on grass, insects, reptiles, rodents, birds, small carnivores, lions, leopard, black rhino, white rhino, hippo, elephant, zebra, waterbuck, kudu, buffalo, bushbuck, grysbok, pangolin, man and even their own dead. In settled areas where there is little other food they may take to stock killing. The hunting and feeding habits of hyaenas vary from area to area in accordance with locally prevailing conditions — habitat type, availability of water causing game to concentrate or disperse, species and age structure of the game population. When feeding off a large animal such as giraffe, buffalo or rhino, spotted hyaenas gather in large numbers, and there is much snapping at one another, social greetings and the excited giggles and howls for which hyaenas are well known. They will try and grab as much food as they can and either swallow it on the spot or run away with it to feed, away from the distraction of the other hyaenas that will try and take it from them. Indigestible remains of their prey such as hooves and hair may be regurgitated or passed through as faeces. The droppings of hyaenas generally turn white as they dry because of the high proportion of calcium from the bones which they consume. They used to clear the refuse in Cape Town in the 18th century and have been known to feed on humans when the opportunity presented itself. Spotted hyaenas are generally wary of man, but in some areas have been known to attack people sleeping in the open, usually biting the face. In some parks they have become accustomed to tourist traffic and have taken to begging food, which inconsiderate visitors readily provide. This practice invariably leads to the visitors being bitten and the hyaenas being destroyed and is most undesirable. Also recorded chewing on car tyres and are well known for pinching utensils from camps.

HABITS

Spotted hyaenas generally live in family groups led by a female, or clans of up to 15 animals which share the same clan range and sleeping dens. The dens may be in old antbear diggings, dongas, rocky outcrops, thickets or more recently even in man-made culverts and drain pipes. There is a strong social fabric and females dominate the males. Spotted hyaenas have developed an elaborate greeting ceremony in which the genitalia are mutually presented by the raising of the one hind leg as the two animals stand parallel to one another but facing opposite directions. The animals then sniff at the exposed genitals. This is accompanied by appeasement activities, especially when young animals are greeting larger animals, and the submissive animal will then fall on to its side while exposing the genitals for inspection. It is thought that this behaviour has evolved to distract the hyaena from the dangerous end of the other animal and so to minimise fighting and biting with the formidable teeth and jaws possessed by this species.

Each hyaena clan has a territory over which it ranges in nightly foraging expeditions. The boundaries of the clan area are marked by secretions from anal glands which are pasted on to grass stems and by communal latrines. The boundaries are patrolled by the clan members and pitched battles occur with intruders or neighbouring clans. The spotted hyaena is well known for its familiar whooping call, which starts on a low note and then rises swiftly up the scale to end abruptly or to tail off into silence. These calls are made by foraging animals and are probably a means of signalling their presence to other members of the clan and to outsiders. The giggling sounds made between competing animals at kills and at carcasses attract the rest of the clan to the food source. Hyaenas are active mainly at night and spend most of the day resting near the den or underground. In hot weather they are often seen lying in water.

BREEDING

There is no pair bond in the spotted hyaena and only one male mates with the oestrous female. Cubs (1-3 in a litter, usually 2) are born after a gestation period of about 100 days. At birth the eyes are open, the cubs weigh about 1,5 kg and they are black with long silky fur. The young depend on their mother's milk for about 8 months and they are not weaned until they are about a year old. By this time they will be following the mother to kills, having spent most of their first few months around the den. The site of the den may be changed from time to time during the period that the cubs are still dependent on it. The adult pelage starts to develop at about six weeks and the cubs are well spotted by four months, though their legs remain dark for up to a year. Hyaenas do not generally have a breeding season and cubs may be born throughout the year.

ENEMIES AND DISEASE

Hyaenas are sometimes killed by lions when venturing too close to a kill. They may possibly also be injured by prey animals defending their young, especially if the attack is made by only one or two hyaenas. They are susceptible to a number of parasitic and disease conditions such as the nematodes *Trichinella spiralis,* which can cause emaciation and paralysis. Various tapeworms are also associated with hyaenas and they have been known to contract rabies. In farming areas they are eliminated by poisoned baits.

BROWN HYAENA
Hyaena brunnea Thunberg, 1820

A: Bruin hiëna, strandwolf, strandjut

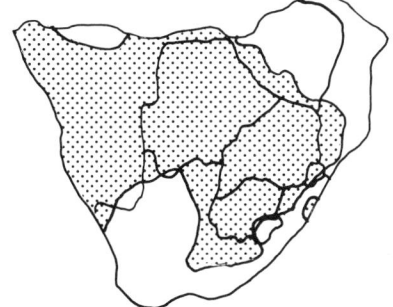

DESCRIPTION

This species is slightly smaller than the spotted hyaena but has a much more shaggy coat, which forms a dense mantle on the back and shoulders and gives it an illusion of size. The ears are large and pointed and the muzzle short. The legs are striped black and buff and the tail is short, bushy and dark. The body colour is a dark chocolate to blackish brown while the longer hairs of the mantle are more tawny or dirty yellow. Like the spotted hyaena, this species also has high forequarters and a sloping back. The brown hyaena stands about 65–88 cm at the shoulder, weighs about 35–55 kg and has a body length of 110–129 cm with a tail 20–25 cm long.

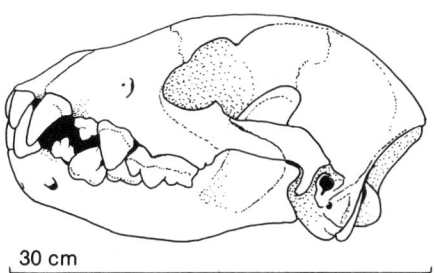

30 cm

DISTRIBUTION AND HABITAT

The brown hyaena is predominantly an animal of the arid western and south-western parts of the interior of Southern Africa. It reaches across into south-western Zimbabwe and as far east as Zinave in Mozambique (from whence doubtful records have come). It is widespread but in low numbers across the central highveld of South Africa and south-east into the eastern Cape. It was well known in the Kruger Park earlier this century, but there have been few recent records. Even in conservation and wilderness areas where the habitat is ideal it is sparsely but widely distributed and individuals move over large areas. It occupies a wide range of habitats from barren Namib beaches to the relatively moist interior grasslands and savanna of the Transvaal.

FEEDING BEHAVIOUR

The brown hyaena is primarily a solitary, nocturnal scavenger, detecting much of its food through an acute sense of smell and hearing. It seldom kills its own prey under

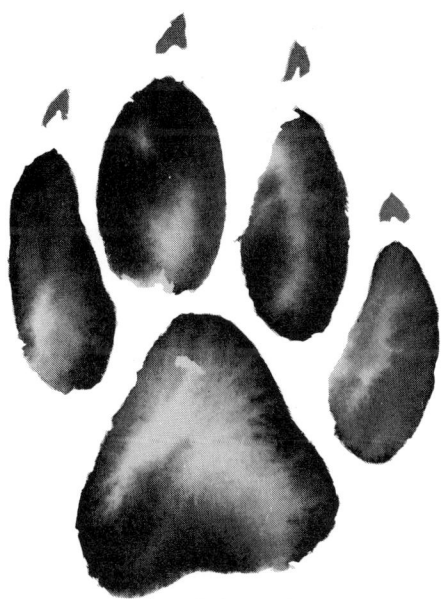

4/5 Actual Size
Forefoot

natural conditions, but reputedly takes to stock killing in settled areas with no game. In addition to scavenging the fresh kills of other large predators — from the smallest to the largest available — it supplements its diet by hunting small mammals (spring-hares, hares, rodents, small canids, klip-springer, dassies) and takes birds and their eggs, insects, fruits, old bones, horns, predator scats and reptiles. Along the beaches of SWA/Namibia and the north-western Cape they scavenge the remains of dead marine animals and also take dead fur-seal pups. Ostrich nests are raided in the Kalahari and the eggs consumed. Brown hyaenas can live independently of surface water, though they occasionally drink when water is available. In their foraging expeditions they may cover great distances every night. The mother and other adults carry food to the cubs while they are still small and remain in a den. When a brown hyaena comes across a large dead animal it may remove parts to store in safe places for later collection and consumption, usually within 24 hours.

HABITS

The brown hyaena is generally a solitary animal, but for all that it is not asocial. Several animals, generally a female and her offspring and other related individuals, will share a territory. In this respect they function as an extended family unit, rather than as the clan of the spotted hyaena. The size of the territory over which the animals range, and thus the number of brown hyaena it can support, depends on the food resources of the area. Generally, the more abundant the food sources, the smaller the range needs to be. Brown hyaenas sharing a territory are generally of different ages and both sexes. When animals of the same sex from adjoining territories meet up they are aggressive and will engage in ritualised fighting. Animals of the opposite sex are more tolerant of one another. Most of the animals occupying a territory will assist in raising the cubs and will bring food to the den to feed them.

The brown hyaena has a greeting cere-mony which is performed by members of the same territory when they meet and presumably has evolved to strengthen the social bonds between the territory's occupants. If they meet at a carcass which is large enough to provide food for more than one animal, they may feed together peacefully, otherwise the dominant animal will appropriate the food.

Much of the communication between brown hyaenas is by scent. The boundaries of the territory are marked by pasting secretions from the anal glands on to grass stems. These are particularly abundant near regularly used sites like latrines and along pathways. The pastings contain a complex mixture of strong-smelling substances and impart information on the occupancy of the territory and the identity of the paster, to other hyaenas. In keeping with its solitary life style and well-developed scent communication, the brown hyaena does not have the communicating

---

Opposite
Top: Foraging brown hyaenas compete with other predators for carcasses.

Below: Brown hyaenas have pointed ears, a dark coat and a pale tawny ruff.

Overleaf
Top: The sloping hindquarters, powerful neck and dark spots of the spotted hyaena are conspicuous features.

Below: The spotted hyaena, unlike the brown hyaena, has rounded ears.

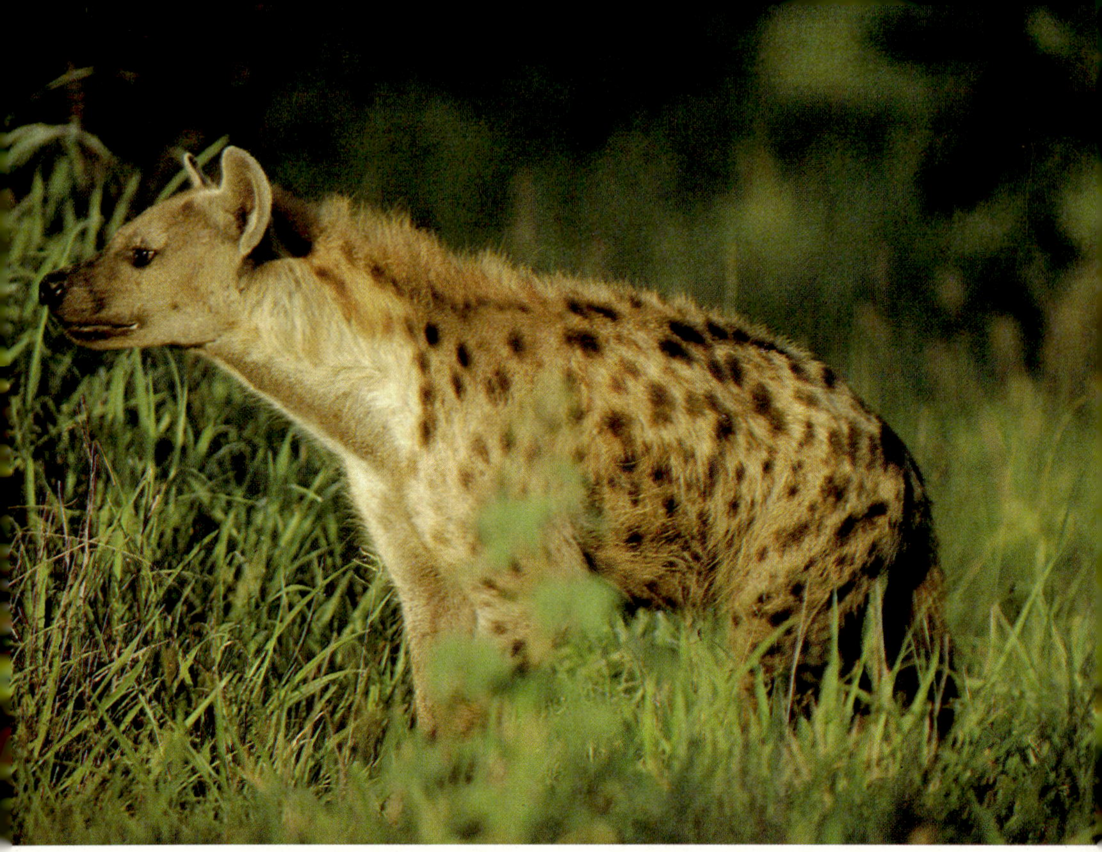

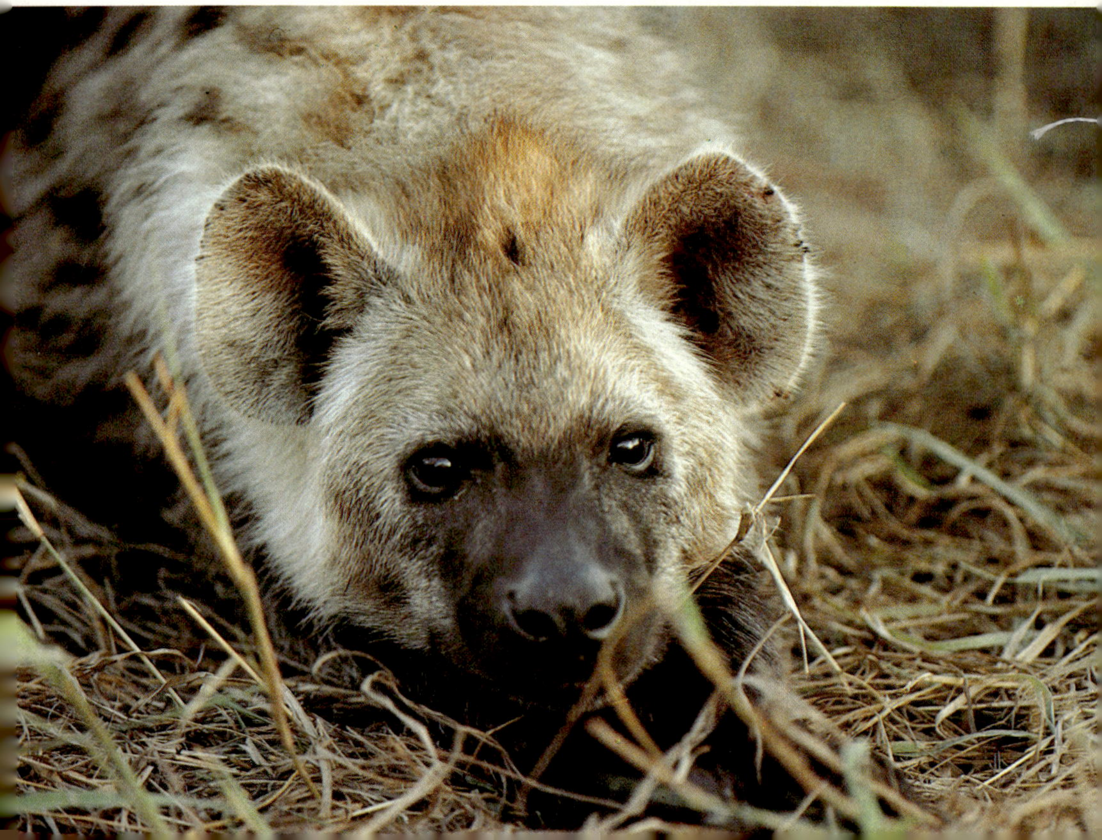

whoop of the spotted hyaena and is generally a silent animal. Being active at night, they rest up during the day in shaded spots under thickets or bushes, in dens underground (usually old antbear holes), or even in caves.

BREEDING

There is no strong pair bond in the brown hyaena and the females are often mated by wandering males that pass through their territory. Cubs (2-4 in a litter) are born after a gestation period of 90 days. The cubs are born with their eyes closed and they open after about four weeks. The cubs remain in the den area, taking only milk for at least three months, whereafter the diet is supplemented by food brought to the den. Like the young of the spotted hyaena, brown hyaena cubs have a long period of dependence on the mother and other members of the extended family who care for them. They start foraging on their own from about 10 months, are weaned at about 12 months but are attached to the den for at least 15 months, by which time they can fend for themselves. A female can come into oestrus again when her cubs are about 9 months old.

ENEMIES AND DISEASE

Brown hyaenas have been persecuted as stock killers and wiped out over large parts of their range. They are often killed by 'coyote getters' which are set in small stock-raising areas for black-backed jackals. In the wild they are occasionally killed by lions and may also suffer in competition with the larger and more aggressive spotted hyaena. High densities of spotted hyaenas are probably the main reason for their virtual absence from areas like the Kruger National Park and Hluhluwe Game Reserve.

Previous page: Spotted hyaena are born black and start changing to the adult colouration at about six weeks.

Opposite: Aardwolf pups are born with adult colouration.

AARDWOLF
Proteles cristatus Sparrman, 1783

A: Aardwolf, maanhaarjakkals

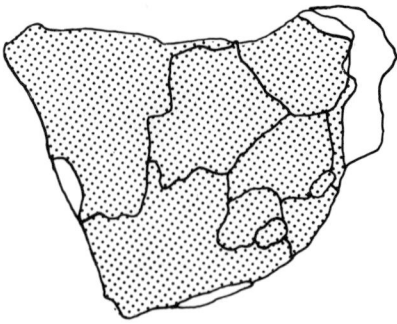

DESCRIPTION

This is a medium-sized carnivore, which closely resembles the striped hyaena of north-east Africa. The ears are pointed and quite large, the face is quite flat and dark, and the rest of the body a pale buff or reddish-brown with distinct black lines running vertically down the body and around the legs, which are slightly darker than the upper parts. The tail is bushy, lacks stripes and is dark at the end. The aardwolf has a well-developed mane which runs from the neck along the back into the tail. As can be seen from the skull drawing, the cheek teeth are reduced and very poorly developed, while the canines, probably used in fighting, are well developed. It has a sloping back much the same as in the hyaena, stands about 50 cm at the shoulder and has a body mass of about 11 kg. Head and body measure 59–89 cm, while the tail is 21–26 cm long.

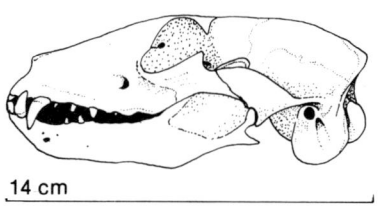

14 cm

DISTRIBUTION AND HABITAT

This animal shows a very wide habitat tolerance, from fairly dense woodland areas to the arid Namib desert, and is consequently found virtually throughout the region except in the more developed areas.

FEEDING BEHAVIOUR

The aardwolf is a highly specialised carnivore adapted to feeding on termites, especially from the *Trinervitermes* and *Hodotermes* genera. The ears are used to locate the termites which are then lapped up with the tongue; a large amount of soil is also ingested in the process. The termites are licked from the surface of the soil while those taken by the antbear (which is also a specialised termite eater) are taken from below the surface. The aardwolf will often feed on termites exposed by the digging of antbears. Despite a strong predilection for

Actual Size

termites, the aardwolf will also occasionally feed on other food items such as carrion, small rodents, millipedes, and other insects such as ants, beetles, fly larvae and bugs. These animals are a real asset to any farmer.

HABITS

These animals are nocturnal but may occasionally be seen at dusk, or even earlier on overcast days. They normally spend the daylight hours in old antbear holes or similar refuges and sometimes lie up in long grass or a small bush. In colder regions they have been seen lying up in a patch of sun next to a bush and not far from the burrow. Several burrows may be used alternately in a home range occupied by at least two individuals. Within such a home range are several latrines or dung middens which are visited nightly while in use. The droppings are large for the size of the animal and are buried in the latrine, the older deposits being exposed in the process. Latrines are often situated on old termitaria which are eventually completely flattened. Near these latrines one may find tiny sticky brown spots on grass stems: these are secretions from the anal glands and serve to mark the area. Marking is a frequent event while foraging and is done by the animal in a squatting position in the same way as is done by hyaenas. The secretion smells of formic acid. When threatened an aardwolf will growl loudly and erect its mane, thus giving the appearance of an animal twice the size. Aardwolves also bark sharply and produce a musky smell when under stress.

BREEDING

One to three young are born in burrows after a gestation period of about 60 days. They are born during the summer months. At birth the eyes are closed, but the pups have a dense covering of hair with distinct stripes as in the adults, while lacking the crest on the back. While still small the young are sometimes carried by the scruff of the neck, in the mouth of their mother, to new dens.

ENEMIES AND DISEASE

They may contract rabies, but appear to play no part in the maintenance of the disease. Some are killed by vehicles as they appear quite unable to take avoiding action when caught in the headlights of a car. Aardwolves are also preyed on by leopards.

CATS

The cats are a specialised group of carnivores with shortened skulls and a reduced number of teeth. The canines are well developed for killing, while the cheek teeth are modified for cutting rather than chewing. All except the cheetah have fully retractable claws which are large, sharp and particularly well developed on the front paws. The hind feet have only four toes and are usually smaller than the front ones. There are seven species of cats in the region and they vary greatly in size from the lion to the black-footed cat. The others are the African wild cat, serval, caracal, leopard and cheetah.

AFRICAN WILD CAT
Felis lybica Forster, 1780

E: Cape wild cat. *A:* Groukat, vaal-boskat

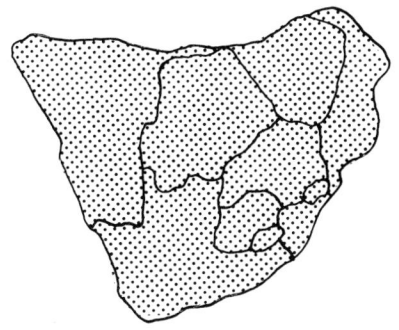

DESCRIPTION
These cats are similar in appearance to domestic cats but are larger, and stand high on the legs. As they readily hybridise with domestic cats, there are a variety of colours to be found in the wild. The typical colour of a true African wild cat is a speckly grey with black bands on the legs and tail, the underparts being pale grey to white and the back of the ears reddish-brown. Adult males stand about 35 cm at the shoulder, have head and body measurements of 46–66 cm, a tail 25–35 cm long and a mass of up to 5 kg.

DISTRIBUTION AND HABITAT
They are widespread throughout the region and show a wide habitat tolerance from the Kalahari desert to moist woodland.

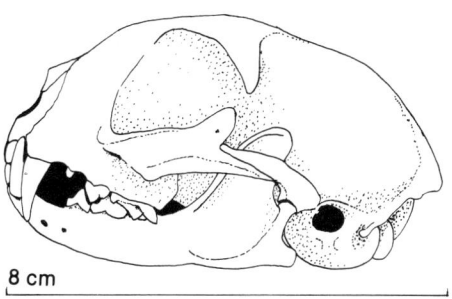

8 cm

FEEDING BEHAVIOUR
Their main food consists of small rodents and they take a wide variety of these, but they are also fond of birds and can become avid poultry thieves. In the wild they take mainly the smaller birds but have been recorded as feeding on birds as large as korhaans. They are also recorded as feeding on the larger of the small mammals such as squirrels, hares and springhares. Their diet includes a variety of insects, centipedes, scorpions, sun spiders, spiders, certain fruits, frogs and reptiles including lizards, geckos and snakes.

Actual Size

HABITS
This cat is largely nocturnal but may be seen in daylight in more remote areas where they are undisturbed. Although predominantly terrestrial, they readily climb trees. During the day they hide in thickets and, as they are solitary by nature, can quietly slip away from danger if need be. They may also take refuge in hollow trees, rock crevices and areas with loose boulders. They tame readily but never really lose their wildness and cannot be expected to behave entirely as do domestic cats. They sometimes venture into urban areas where a good deal of cross-breeding with domestic cats takes

place. With the spread and increasing numbers of feral domestic cats in South Africa, the wild populations of pure African wild cats are in danger of becoming hybridised.

BREEDING

One to five young are born after a gestation period of about 58 days, in a suitable lair and mostly during the summer months. The female takes care of the kittens.

ENEMIES AND DISEASE

These cats are preyed on by larger predators including the caracal and the leopard, and could be taken by some of the larger birds of prey. The remains of one has been found in the nest of a bateleur but this may have been taken as carrion. They are considered an important rabies host in some areas and a number are destroyed in control exercises. A small number are killed annually as poultry thieves.

BLACK-FOOTED CAT
Felis nigripes Burchell, 1824

E: Small spotted cat. *A:* Swartpoot-katjie, miershooptier

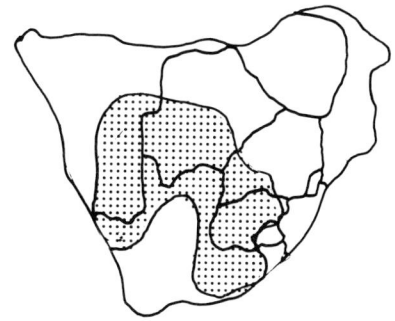

DESCRIPTION

This species is sometimes mistaken for the African wild cat but is quite different in colour, size and shape. The black-footed cat is a small, compact animal with relatively short legs, short tail, large eyes and oval ears. The overall body colour is tawny, with black spots and black bars on the legs, chest and tail. It stands only about 25 cm at the shoulder, has head and body measurements of 41–49 cm, a tail length of 15–20 cm and a body mass of up to 2 kg. The canines appear particularly long and sharp for the size of the animal.

DISTRIBUTION AND HABITAT

This small cat is fairly uncommon and is found in the semi-arid scrub veld of southern SWA/Namibia, southern and central Botswana, south-western Transvaal, Orange Free State, northern Cape and the north-eastern Cape as far south as the valley bushveld of the Addo Elephant National Park near Port Elizabeth. It appears to favour the more open country and is less inclined to live in the hills.

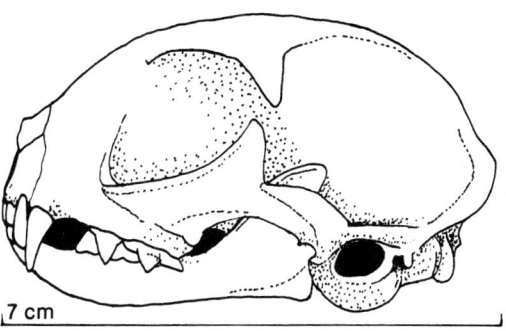

7 cm

FEEDING BEHAVIOUR

Black-footed cats feed on a variety of small rodents, ground birds up to the size of a courser, and invertebrates such as spiders, sun spiders and insects, including beetles, grasshoppers and moths. They will also eat small insectivores such as elephant shrews, and lizards.

Actual Size

HABITS

These small cats make up for their size by being extremely vicious: they will attack with teeth and claws when cornered, snarling, spitting and hissing. Solitary and nocturnal, they take refuge in dense scrub or holes in the ground such as old termitaria, thus the Afrikaans name of *miershooptier* (anthill tiger). Very little else is known about them. Apparently, they do not tame at all in captivity.

BREEDING

Up to three young are born in a litter, mostly in the summer months. The young are born in a hole in the ground about two metres deep and are cared for by the female.

ENEMIES AND DISEASE

They are likely to be taken on occasion by larger predators and large birds of prey. The incidence of rabies in this species is low.

Opposite: The African wild cat is a hunter of small game including francolin.

Overleaf: Typical field criteria of the black-footed cat are the distinct spots, short tail and round ears.

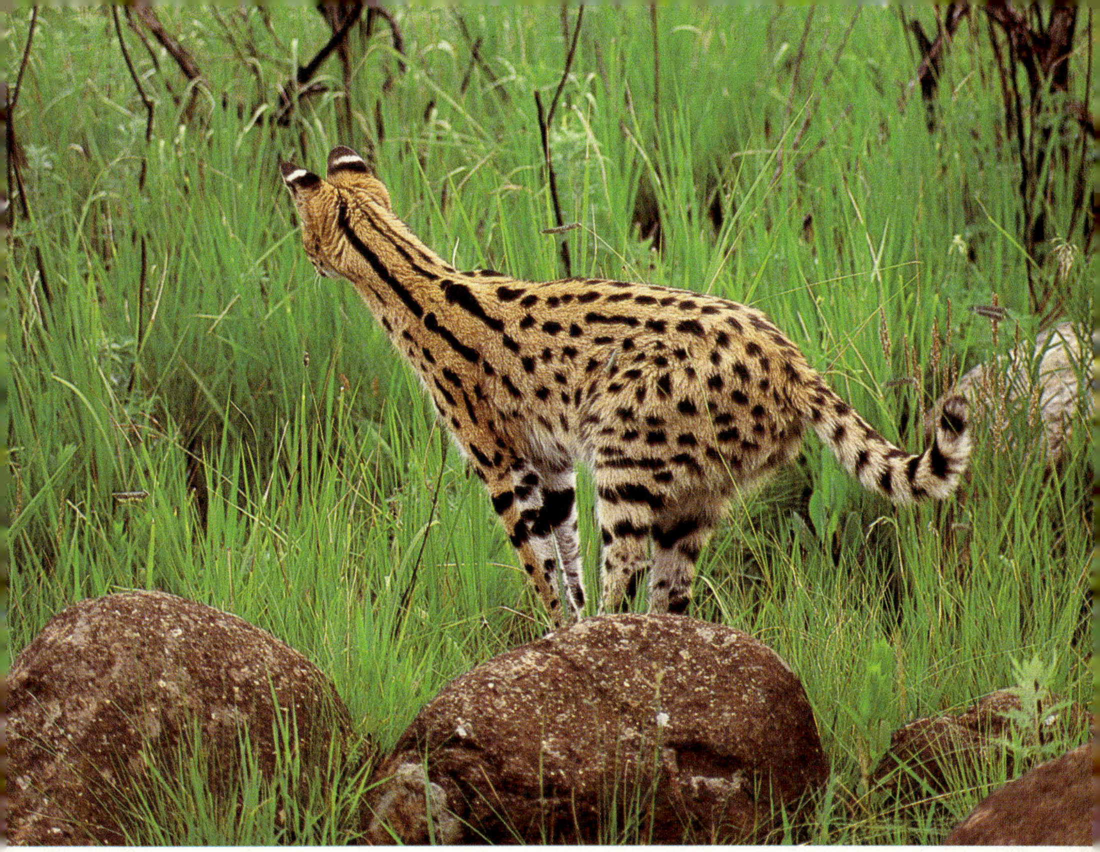

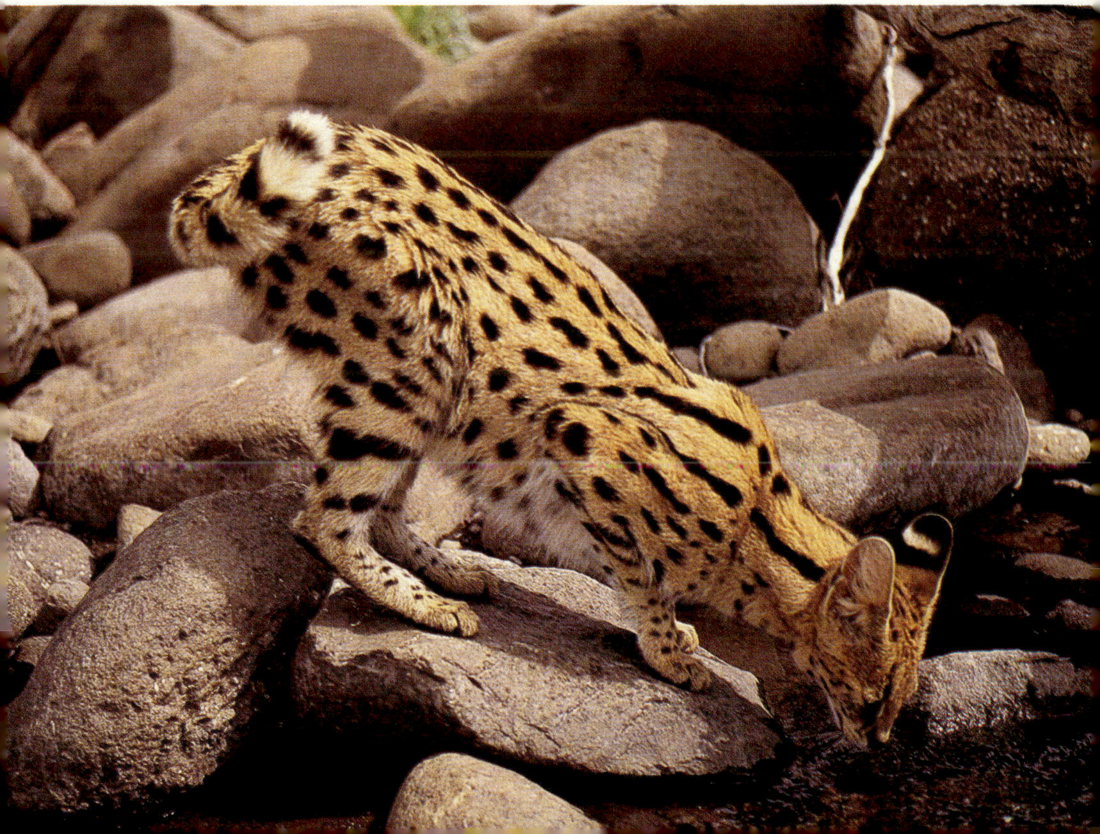

SERVAL
Felis serval Schreber, 1776

A: Tierboskat

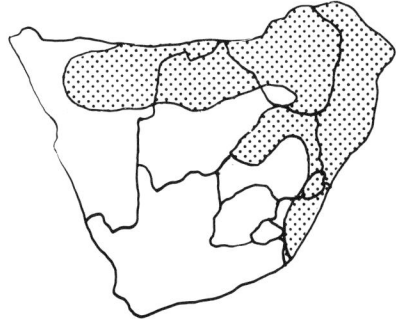

DESCRIPTION

Superficially, this cat resembles the leopard and the cheetah but, apart from being smaller, it has a relatively short tail (24–30 cm), large ears and elongated markings on the back. The overall body colour is a golden brown with large black spots scattered over the entire body, black rings around the tail and very variable, elongated markings along the back. The back of the ear is brown at the base, the top half being black with a white 'eye' in the centre. The spots on the face are small with a slight black streak running through the eye, and the throat is generally unmarked. It has a shoulder height of about 55 cm, head and body measurement of 65–100 cm and a mass of up to 14 kg.

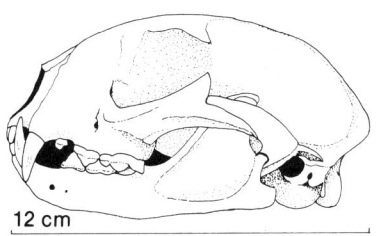

12 cm

DISTRIBUTION AND HABITAT

These animals are widely but sparsely distributed in Mozambique, Zimbabwe, northern Botswana, north-eastern SWA/Namibia, and eastern Transvaal south to the western regions of Natal. Apparently they were found along the Cape coastal belt in the past, but the latest information indicates that this is no longer so. The serval shows preference for higher-rainfall areas with long grass, reedbeds and vleis.

FEEDING BEHAVIOUR

Serval feed mainly on small rodents, particularly vleirats, which are associated with moist conditions. Prey is often located by the large ears listening for movement, the paws are then used to strike down on the prey. The serval generally take much

Actual Size

Previous page
Top: The back of the serval's ear is brown at the base, with a white 'eye' in the centre.
Below: A serval drinking; Bushmans River, Giants Castle.
Opposite: The powerfully built caracal has distinctive black tassles to its ears.

smaller prey than the caracal and have small paws in comparison. They will also feed on other small mammals such as shrews, hares, canerats, the young of small antelope, birds, reptiles, frogs and a variety of invertebrates such as insects (beetles, grasshoppers, moths) and sun spiders. They may take poultry but this is rare. When eating birds they feed on the head first in the same way as genets.

HABITS

Mainly nocturnal and solitary, but may be seen at dusk in areas where they are undisturbed, and are sometimes encountered in pairs or a female with young forming a family group. They are predominantly terrestrial but can climb readily when necessary. During the day they lie up in thickets or long grass from which they are sometimes flushed, and will at times take refuge in old antbear holes. They become quite tame in captivity and in some areas of Zimbabwe may be found close to human habitation. In defence they arch the back, spitting loudly and growling. They also growl while feeding in captivity and kittens utter a call similar to the chirp of a cheetah. The kittens are also said to utter a sharp 'cheoo' sound at intervals, and tame animals will purr. There are no records of these animals feeding on domestic stock and they are a useful species to have around.

BREEDING

Up to three young are born in summer but the breeding season may be extended over several months. The young are born in lairs such as antbear holes, but a very young kitten was once found in dense tall grassveld. The young, which are born after a gestation period of 60–70 days, have a paler ground colour than the adults with indistinct dark spots.

ENEMIES AND DISEASE

The serval is likely to fall prey to larger carnivores and in the Matopos (Zimbabwe) one was found killed by a leopard but not eaten. Rarely associated with rabies.

CARACAL
Felis caracal (Schreber, 1776)

E: African lynx. *A:* Rooikat

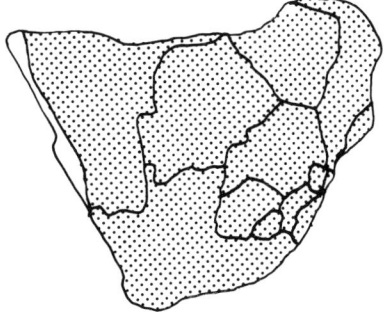

DESCRIPTION

These animals are easily recognisable, being of medium build with powerful legs and a short tail. The overall body colour is red-brown with tiny white flecks, the underparts are paler, almost white with faint brown spots. Southern animals are much darker than their northern counterparts. The ears have characteristic long black tufts at the tip, the back of the ears being black with white hairs interspersed. The face is beautifully marked with a white chin, black upper lips and a black line running vertically through the eye. They stand about 45 cm at the shoulder and have a mass of up to 20 kg in the males. Females are lighter, with a mass of up to 14 kg. Head and body measurements are 70–105 cm, and tail length 19–34 cm.

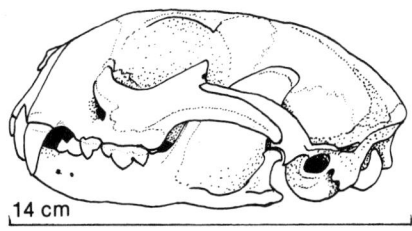

14 cm

DISTRIBUTION AND HABITAT

This species is widely distributed throughout the region and is perhaps more common in some areas than generally believed. They have a wide habitat tolerance and are found from the coastal forests of Knysna, through the Karoo to the moist savanna woodland areas of the north. They occur at high densities in the broken hilly country of the Karoo regions, particularly in the north-eastern Cape.

Actual Size

FEEDING BEHAVIOUR

The caracal is an opportunistic feeder, adapted to living under varying conditions and quite capable of killing prey much larger than itself. They feed mainly on mammals but will also take birds, reptiles and, to a lesser extent, invertebrates. Where they occur in the same habitat as dassies, these small herbivores form the main part of their diet and in the north-eastern Cape where they occur with mountain reedbuck, these antelope are commonly taken. Large rams of this species with a mass of 35 kg are readily killed by the caracal. Apart from various small rodents, a wide range of mammalian prey is recorded for the species, including steenbok, duiker, springbok, impala, grysbok, small kudu, dune molerat, scrub hare, red rock hare, springhare and even carnivores such as black-backed jackal, Cape grey mongoose, bat-eared fox and African wild cat. Unfortunately, small stock such as sheep and goats fall within the size range of prey taken by caracals and they have become a problem in many parts of the Cape. What aggravates the situation further is that sheep are rather stupid and tend to stand around after the first one is killed, which can result in the caracal killing numerous others.

Larger prey species are killed with a bite to the throat, usually after a careful stalk culminating in a fast rush. The powerful hindquarters propel the animal forward and the vicious claws on the front feet are often used to hook the prey in order to get a grip with the teeth. Smaller prey may be hit with the forepaws, killed and carried away but larger prey is either left where it was killed or dragged a short distance to the nearest cover. An adult male duiker, for example, was found dragged over a distance of 65 metres, and smaller prey such as spring-hare may at times be taken into a tree. In areas where grass or litter is available the kill is partially covered.

As in the case of the leopard, quite a large amount of hair is plucked from larger kills (using the front teeth) to avoid the consumption of excessive hair. Unlike the leopard though, the caracal does not remove the innards of larger prey but commences feeding on the thick flesh of the hindquarters. Once most of this is consumed they will move to the shoulder and neck region. In certain farming areas they are reputed not to return to their kills after the first night. In all kills examined the innards were not consumed, even with the smaller prey species, except rats, mice and small birds.

HABITS

These cats are largely nocturnal but are sometimes active during the day, particularly in areas where they are undisturbed. They are solitary by nature and groups seen together are generally a female with her young which may be as old as 10 months. During the day they will lie up in thickets or rock crevices and, although they are largely terrestrial, they climb with amazing speed.

Young males wander widely, while older males appear to establish territories encompassing the hunting range of one or two females. They will fight viciously when cornered and females surprised with kittens have been known to attack humans. When threatened they will growl, hiss loudly and spit. A threat display with a tame male was an arched back with the teeth fully bared. They will purr when relaxed and become quite tame in captivity if reared from an early age. Kittens and young adults have been heard using a bird-like communication call. The dung is not generally deposited in the same place in the wild, but several deposits of varying age may be found on the same site. The deposits are not covered.

BREEDING

Up to four young are born after a gestation period of about 76 days and breeding appears to take place during most months of the year but mainly in summer. The young are born with closed eyes which open from six to ten days old, the ears are pitch black and folded down. The young kittens are also a dark red colour which changes with age. They are born in lairs which range from a dense bush on a hill slope to a rock crevice. The female rears the young and they will accompany her on a hunt when only a few months old. If a female is disturbed in captivity after she has given birth, she may eat her young, as will many other carnivores.

ENEMIES AND DISEASE

These animals may at times be taken by larger carnivores and the remains of one has been found at a martial eagle's nest. Black eagles will swoop down on caracals in their territory and may well take the young. Black-backed jackals are said to take the young of caracal but there is no evidence to substantiate this. The caracal's major enemy is man and many hundreds, at times thousands, are killed annually in the small-stock farming areas of the Cape. In spite of this, the species seems to be holding its own and even increasing in certain areas.

LION
Panthera leo (Linnaeus, 1758)

A: Leeu

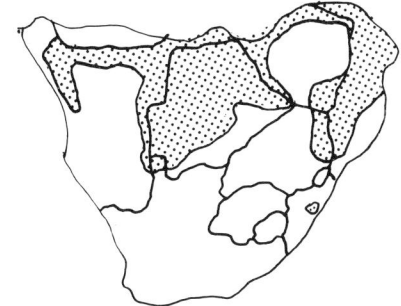

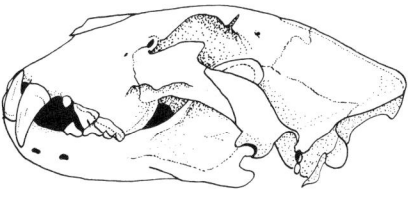

45 cm

DESCRIPTION

The most imposing and largest of the African carnivores with a powerfully built, muscular body, lions are among the few carnivore species in which there is a marked difference between the sexes. The adult male has an impressive blond, ginger or black mane on his neck which can extend on to his shoulders and belly. The lioness is a sleeker-looking, smaller animal with no mane. The total length of a lion from nose to tail tip may be as much as 2,5–3,3 m and that of females 2,3–2,7 m, of which the tail may make up 100 cm. Lions in Southern Africa stand about 120 cm at the shoulder, and lionesses about 105 cm. They are larger than lions elsewhere in Africa. Adult males weigh 150–225 kg and females 110–152 kg. The long tail has a conspicuous tuft of long, blackish hairs and the tip has a curious horny hook to it. The overall colour of the short soft coat varies from tawny gold to honey brown to grey, with paler (almost white in the case of females) bellies and the insides of the legs. The ears are small, rounded and black-tipped behind. Subtle colour patterns emphasise facial expressions and are an essential part of visual communication; pale markings around the eyes contrast strongly with the black lids and the deep amber to yellow eyes, while the dark lips are set against a whitish muzzle and chin. The claws, as in most cats, can be sheathed or exposed at will. Cubs have a woolly fur with dark rosette-like spotting on the flanks and legs and these faintly outlined spots usually persist into adulthood in the lioness but not in the lion. White lions are found occasionally in the Tshokwane district of the Kruger National Park. The discovery of three white lion cubs in the Timbavati Nature Reserve some years ago was widely publicised. These lions, generally pure

3/4 Actual Size

white as cubs, darken somewhat to a yellowish colour with age. They are not albinos, but it is believed that an autosomal recessive gene is responsible for this colour variation. Carriers of the white gene may be normally coloured and it is only when two carriers mate that a white lion is produced. Because the white gene is recessive, a white cub may have normal coloured siblings. White lions are normal in all other respects, can hunt and are fully accepted as pride members.

DISTRIBUTION AND HABITAT

Lions are incompatible with human settlement and they now occur only in parks, reserves and in some isolated undeveloped areas, where there are still sufficient popultions of game to serve as a food source. In SWA/Namibia they are now common only in the Etosha National Park, but still occur in Damaraland, Kaokoland, Hereroland and Bushmanland. In Botswana they are still fairly widespread except in the east. In Zimbabwe they are now found mainly in the wildlife areas of the south-west, north-west, the south-eastern lowveld and the Zambezi Valley. In Mozambique they are widespread in the sparsely settled Gaza district and common in the Gorongoza area. In South Africa they are confined to the eastern Transvaal lowveld, the Kalahari Gemsbok National Park and the Hluhluwe/Umfolozi game reserve complex. Wandering animals appear on farms and ranches bordering their range throughout Southern Africa and these are usually quickly destroyed. Lions can adapt to virtually any habitat type from barren sub-desert (as in Damaraland), through shrub thornveld and savanna grassland to lush tropical woodlands. They are not, however, found in forested areas.

FEEDING BEHAVIOUR

The lion is predominantly a hunter of medium- to large-sized mammals. Hunting is a communal effort, with all the members of the pride taking part in some capacity —
though most kills are made by lionesses. Although they will take almost any warm-blooded prey from rodents to young elephants, they do exhibit prey preferences in different areas, partly determined by availability of prey species and a variety of other circumstances. In the Kruger National Park their prey in order of preference is wildebeest, impala, zebra, waterbuck, kudu, giraffe and buffalo. In the Kalahari with its very different habitat (mainly semi-desert shrubland and thornveld) the spectrum of available wildlife and hunting conditions are very different and here gemsbok are the most frequently taken prey, while porcupines are second on the list. There are marked seasonal preference changes in the diet of lions as they can switch their hunting effort to take advantage of whatever prey is most readily available, e.g. wildebeest calves during the early summer period.

Hunting techniques vary according to the density of the vegetation, and the dispersal or concentration of game in relation to waterholes. The hunt consists of a search (during which the pride may move long distances together or well spread out), a stalk once the potential prey has been spotted or heard (rather than scented — scent plays little role in detecting live prey), a short charge or chase once the lion has approached to within range or is detected by the prey, and the kill. If the hunted animal can avoid the charge, the lion does not chase it very far and soon gives up. Different killing techniques are also used: thus wildebeest in the Kruger Park are usually killed by breaking the neck or holding the animal down and suffocating it by biting into the throat or by holding the muzzle in the lion's mouth. When gemsbok, with their dangerous rapier-like horns, are tackled, the kill is made by approaching from behind out of reach of the horns and breaking the animal's back. Large animals such as buffalo, hippo and giraffe are usually tackled only when several lions act together, while smaller animals are killed by single lions. Other prey items include zebra, eland, waterbuck, warthog, kudu, sable and roan antelope, reedbuck, tsessebe, baboon, antbear, rhino, bushbuck, bushpig, duiker, red hartebeest, lechwe, puku, nyala, steenbok, Sharpe's grysbok, klipspringer, lion, hyaena, leopard, cheetah, jackal, civet, honey badger, caracal, pangolin, ostrich, crocodile, snake, tortoise, domestic stock, chickens and dogs. Lions will also scavenge. Opinions vary as to whether lions cooperate in hunting to the extent of laying an ambush, with some members of the pride chasing game to waiting lions. It seems more likely that lions spread out in a stalk and make the best use of whatever situation develops once the game is disturbed and stampedes.

Lions drink regularly when water is available and usually after every meal. In semi-desert areas they may go for long periods without drinking, presumably deriving sufficient moisture from their prey. They are well known as man-eaters in many parts, usually being forced into this situation by an injury, old age or starvation.

HABITS

Lions are the most sociable of cats, living in fairly cohesive prides which may number 4–30 animals. The density in the Kalahari Gemsbok National Park is one lion in 68,5 sq. km, in north-west Zimbabwe (Matetse) it is about one lion in 16 sq. km, in the central district of Kruger National Park it is one in eight and in parts of Kenya as high as one in 2,6 sq. km. One or two large males, often even three or four, dominate the pride, which further consists of several adult females, some sub-adults and cubs of various ages. Pride size varies according to the availability of food — when food is abundant and easily taken, cub survival is high and the prides tend to be larger. Conversely, during times of food shortage, or difficult hunting conditions such as during extremely wet years when game may be well dispersed, cub survival may be low, lionesses may not come into oestrus and pride size will decline. Sub-adult males disperse away from the area occupied by the parental pride and either take up a nomadic

existence following game, or find a vacant area which they can occupy. The pride area or territory is defended against strange lions by both males and females. The boundaries are clearly marked by the residents spraying urine on bushes, scratching the ground, and by latrine sites. These actions leave visible and chemical indicators to other lions that the territory is occupied. In addition the lion is capable of producing an immense volume of sound when roaring. A full roar can be heard by humans up to 8 km away on a still night and probably much further than that by other lions, and it is a very effective means of advertising the presence of the territorial pride.

Lions are most active at night, and that is the time when most kills are made, though they also hunt in the early morning and late afternoon. During the day they rest in shady spots under trees or in the dense vegetation of thickets or reedbeds — they are also not averse to lying in the open especially on a cool day. In some areas they are bothered by biting flies and will then take to the trees, but this is not usual. Their resting postures are immensely variable — and all seem eminently comfortable to the human observer. They lie on their bellies, sides, or even on their backs with their legs spread wide. They may doze and sleep for as much as 15 hours per day. Cubs are extremely playful and their antics are well tolerated by the adults, but there are warnings to cubs which they ignore at their peril and at the risk of being soundly cuffed or snapped at by an adult. There is a great deal of social interaction between members of the pride, and this includes the greeting ceremony and mutual grooming.

Once a kill has been made, the dominant male or males take precedence in feeding, and if there is not sufficient meat for all, then the cubs have to make do with the scraps or go hungry, though sometimes the males allow the cubs to feed while keeping the females away. This seemingly selfish system helps to ensure that lions, the top carnivore of most intact African ecosystems, do not outgrow their food supply. When dominant males are displaced by stronger males, the new males may kill the cubs of their predecessors, who are potential competitors with their own progeny. This stimulates the lioness to come into oestrus and ensures the continuation of the new pride male's genetic strain.

BREEDING

Lions do not have any defined breeding season and lionesses can come into oestrus every few weeks throughout the year, provided they are in good condition. Mating is not confined to one male in a pride where there is more than one dominant lion and consists of numerous couplings over a period of about two days. Mating is accompanied by appropriate communication of intent by means of a 'mating snarl' and ritualised attacks by the lioness on the lion. After a gestation period of about 108 days, 2–6 cubs are born (sometimes more) in a secluded spot in a thicket, long grass or reedbeds. The cubs are hidden at first while the mother hunts, but as they grow older they spend more time with the pride. They are weaned at ten weeks, but they retain a fairly close association with the mother until they are about 18 months old. They learn to hunt and kill from their mother and by playing with their siblings. They become independent by the age of two years.

ENEMIES AND DISEASE

The only significant enemy of the lion is man — who has been hunting, trapping or poisoning lions for thousands of years and has driven them from most of their former range. Old and infirm lions may be killed by hyaenas and even wild dogs, but are just as likely to be dispatched by their own species. Spotted hyaenas can also sometimes take kills away from a lion. Like most carnivores, they are host to a large array of internal parasites such as roundworms and tapeworms. They are also susceptible to rickets and mange.

Lions are vulnerable when they have been injured by their prey or get porcupine quills in their feet or mouths. Under such conditions or when old age and infirmity overtakes them, they may become man-eaters.

Opposite: Caracal kittens venture from the maternal den at an early age.

LEOPARD
Panthera pardus (Linnaeus, 1758)

A: Luiperd

DESCRIPTION

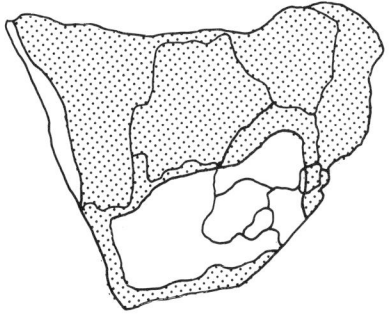

An elegant, powerfully built large cat, the leopard epitomises feline grace. It has a dense soft coat with a buffy, yellowish or whitish ground colour and dark rosettes formed by circles of irregular spots on the back, flanks, rump and upper limbs. The legs are spotted and on the chest the spots coalesce to form several dark bands. The head and shoulder markings consist of dark spots not gathered into rosettes with the nose and upper muzzle not spotted at all. The whiskers are long and white and rise from dark spots regularly arranged in rows on the side of the muzzle. The eyes have generally paler surrounds. The chin, throat, belly and insides of the legs are whitish or dirty yellow with some diffuse spotting. The ears are small and rounded, the back of the ear being outlined in black with a pale almost white centre, presumably acting as focal points for transmitting signals to young leopards following their mother. The rosettes become heavier towards the tip of the usually upcurled tail and the tip is white — also a signalling device. The body is long (104–180 cm) with a long tail (67–110 cm); the legs are relatively short, giving a shoulder height of about 70–80 cm. Males are generally larger and heavier than females, and the leopards of the Cape mountains are generally smaller than those of the savanna areas elsewhere in Southern Africa. Male savanna leopards weigh 40–90 kg and females 30–60 kg, while in the Cape males weigh only 20–45 kg and females 17–26 kg. A striking feature of the leopard is the eyes — they are pale and cold with a somewhat baleful expression.

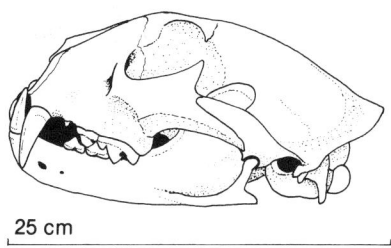

25 cm

Actual Size

Opposite
Top: Lionesses lack the magnificent manes so characteristic of adult male lions.

Below: White lion cubs may have normally coloured litter mates.

DISTRIBUTION AND HABITAT

The leopard, because of its stealthy, solitary way of life and its ability to live on a wide variety of food sources in all habitats from semi-desert shrublands, savanna, rugged mountain fynbos and forests, is still the most widespread of the larger carnivores in Southern Africa. It is found throughout the mountains of the eastern, southern and western Cape and in the Kalahari thornveld of the northern Cape. Leopards are widespread in SWA/Namibia except for the Namib, the south eastern plains and Ovamboland; they occur throughout Botswana and are also well distributed throughout much of Zimbabwe, Mozambique and the sparsely settled bushveld areas of the Transvaal, Swaziland and Zululand. Isolated populations occur elsewhere in Natal.

FEEDING BEHAVIOUR

The leopard is primarily a solitary hunter of small to medium-sized mammals, but it takes a wide range of prey and usually whatever is most readily available. Its hunting technique is a silent stalk, ending in a short rush or pounce to take its prey or bowl it over, and it kills by a bite to the nape of the neck, back of the skull or throat. It also sometimes grasps prey with the forefeet and suffocates it by clamping the mouth over the muzzle of the prey animal. Sharp claws aid in knocking or pulling the prey off balance, in grabbing it and holding it. The leopard prefers antelope such as impala, bushbuck, springbok, steenbok, reedbuck, duiker and the young or females of kudu and waterbuck, young wildebeest, sable, buffalo, roan, and zebra. It has also been recorded killing tsessebe in the Kruger National Park. It also takes tortoises, rodents (rats, mice, springhares, porcupines, canerats), hares; birds such as francolin, guineafowl and ostrich; dassie, monkeys and baboons; jackals and other small carnivores (banded mongoose, civet, genet, serval) and insects. The leopard also kills warthog, bushpig and antbear and has been recorded taking carrion and fish. After making a kill the leopard usually drags it to some sheltered spot before commencing to feed, usually on the rib cage. A great deal of hair is plucked from mammalian prey which is also usually degutted. In the case of larger prey species the intestines are buried. It regularly takes the kill high up into the branches of trees in some areas — presumably as a protection from scavengers and as a means of storage. It will then return to the kill to feed on subsequent occasions — an obvious economy not available to other large carnivores. It can survive in areas with little or no water, but drinks regularly where it is available.

HABITS

The leopard is a solitary, secretive animal. When more than one are seen together, it is usually a mating pair or a mother and young and perhaps exceptionally a pair with young. Leopards are more likely to be active at twilight and during the night, especially in areas where there is human settlement. In wilderness areas they are also active during the day. They normally spend the day resting well hidden, in some secluded, shady spot like a thicket, among jumbled boulders on a rock outcrop, or high up in the branches of large trees or even in antbear burrows. The dappled coat helps the leopard to blend into its surroundings so that it can see its enemies or prey without itself being seen. Male and female leopard will squirt a white liquid from the anal gland to mark an area.

Male leopards defend a territory against other males though they do sometimes have overlapping boundaries. There are many records of fights to the death with trespassing leopards. Females occupy a home range which may overlap the territories of several males. There is no permanent pair bond and associations between male and female are transitory. The boundaries of the territory are regularly patrolled and the presence of the owner advertised by latrines, by harsh rasping calling, by scratching on trees along the boundaries and by leaving the owner's scent from sprayed urine on trees and bushes where other leopards will find it. As they are solitary animals, leopards have to depend upon themselves for grooming and this they do by licking and pawing. Mothers do, however, groom their cubs. Being adept at tree climbing, they use trees for resting, for observation posts and also as a refuge to escape other predators. Females also make the rasping, grunting call and as the rate of calling increases when she is in oestrus, it is likely that this serves to advertise her condition to males. They enjoy rolling on bare patches of sand, animal dung, old rotting carcasses and even oily patches on tarred roads.

BREEDING

After pairing, the male and female leopard go their separate ways, though they may still meet up on occasion while patrolling their respective areas. Females in oestrus will growl and drag their back legs, swaying as if paralysed. After a gestation period of 100 days 2-3 cubs are born. They are very dark with indistinct spots and long woolly fur. Their eyes are closed at birth and they open at about 8-10 days old. The cubs suckle for 6-8 weeks and during the early stage of their cubhood they remain hidden in a den or secluded place, even in hollow trees, while the mother goes hunting. Upon returning to the den area the mother may call the cubs to her with a low panting sound. As the cubs grow older the mother leads them to her kills to feed and they are weaned at three months. Gradually they learn to hunt with her. By the age of 14 months the cubs are fully independent, but because cub mortality is high it is seldom that the whole litter survives to this age. Breeding apparently takes place throughout the year but mainly in the summer months.

ENEMIES AND DISEASE

Leopards have been found to suffer from various internal parasites such as tapeworms, hookworms and roundworms, as well as virus infections. Deaths from anthrax have been recorded and cases of rabies are known. Apart from disease their most dangerous enemy, other than man, is the lion; there are many records of lions killing young and adult leopards. Hyaenas of both species have been reported driving leopards from their kills and appropriating the food; spotted hyaenas have also been reported killing leopard cubs and adults in poor condition. Wild dogs have sometimes chased leopards from a kill. The leopard is, however, also able to turn the tables occasionally and make off with the kill of cheetah, hyaena and wild dog. The dominant males of baboon troops are capable of killing a leopard, providing they act in concert. There are a few records of leopards killed by snakebite and one of being killed by a bushpig. As leopards often take to stock raiding in settled areas, they are frequently shot, trapped, or poisoned. Very occasionally they become man-eaters, usually as a result of old age or infirmity.

CHEETAH
Acinonyx jubatus (Schreber, 1775)

A: Jagluiperd

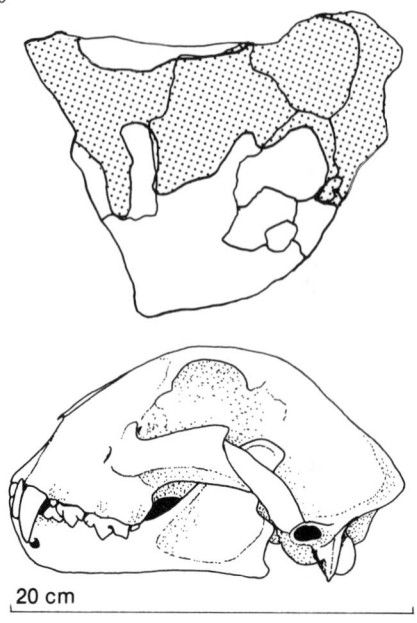

DESCRIPTION

The cheetah is a lean, lithe animal, well adapted for sprinting. It has a small rounded head, thin waist, large chest, long, thick tail used to great effect as a rudder when it turns at speed, and long slender limbs. The coat is whitish to buff and is spotted all over. The spots are black, rounded and of more or less uniform size. There are two distinctive black stripes which run from the eyes to the corner of the mouth and these, in combination with the black lips and dark mouth, combine to accentuate facial expressions which are an integral part of the cheetah's communication mechanisms. The face is flattened and the claws are not retractile like those of the other cats. The ears are short and the hairs on the back of the neck are longer than elsewhere thus forming a slight ruff. The chin, throat, belly and the inside of the legs are whitish and also sparsely spotted; the spots on the tail combine to form bands towards the end and the tip is white. The cheetah stands about 70–90 cm at the shoulder, has a head and body length of 110–150 cm and the tail is about 60–80 cm long. Adults weigh 35–65 kg, males being larger than females. Unlike the long, stabbing canine teeth of the lion and leopard, the cheetah has relatively short canines suited to the cheetah's killing method, which is to clamp on to the throat of its victim and throttle it. Occasionally there are colour variants known as 'King Cheetahs' in which the spots on the back have united to form long broad stripes.

20 cm

4/5 Actual Size

Opposite: A magnificent ginger or dark-coloured mane is characteristic of an adult male lion.

Overleaf
Top: Leopards commonly use the lateral branches of trees as resting sites.

Below: A leopard may sometimes kill by suffocation, the mouth clamped over the muzzle of its prey.

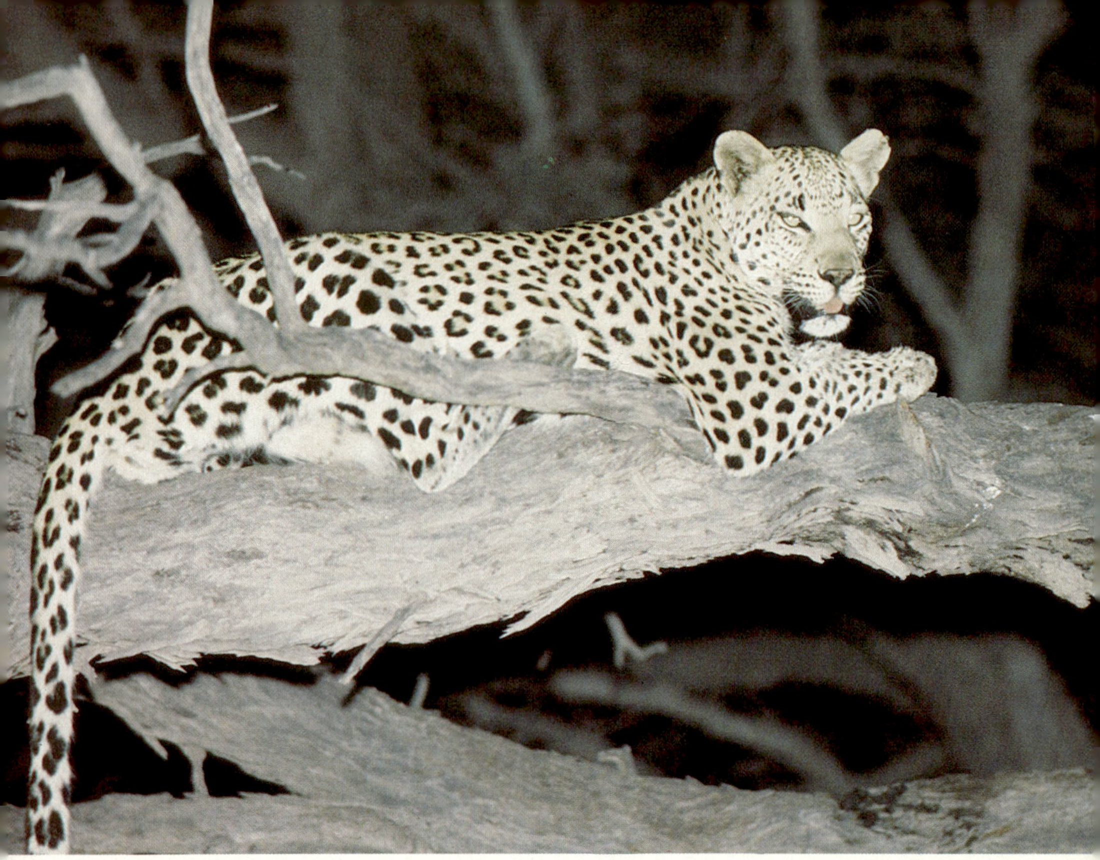

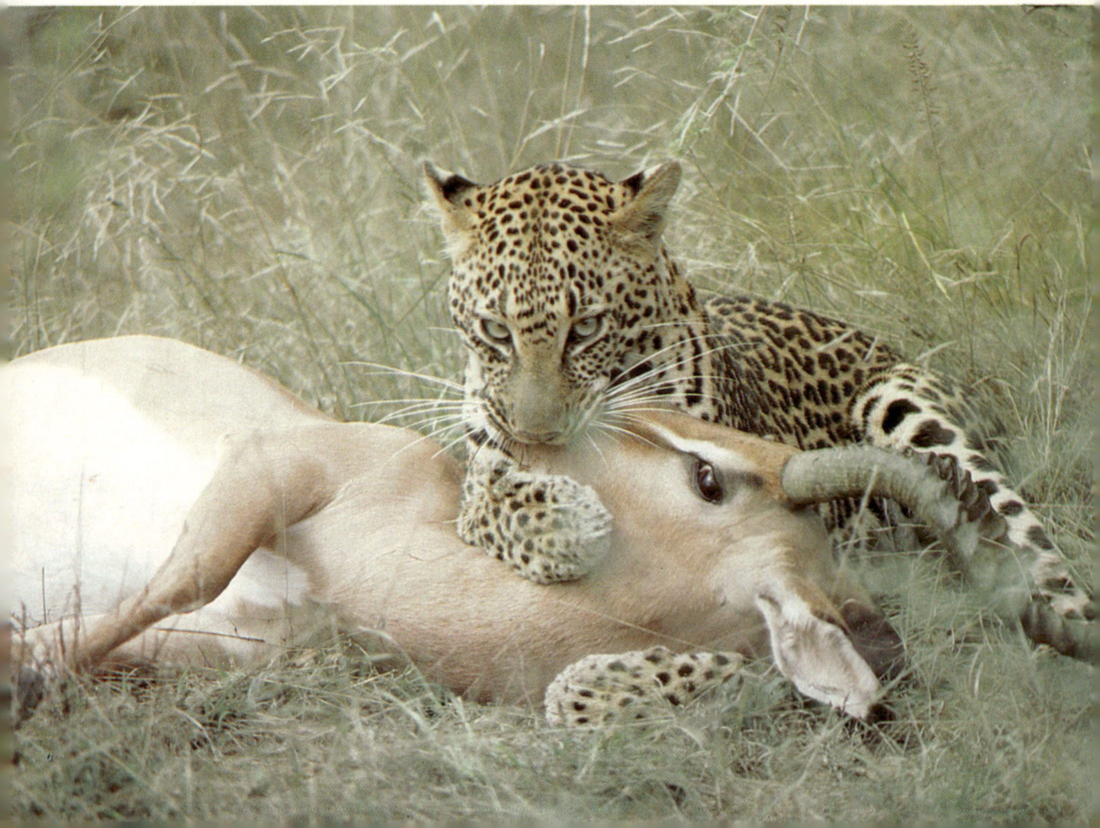

DISTRIBUTION AND HABITAT

Cheetahs are animals of the savannas and open woodlands where visibility is good, suitable prey can be coursed and they can hide. They are, however, equally able to survive in relatively densely wooded country. They generally avoid mountainous country and densely vegetated areas like riverine bush except as places of refuge. They are widely distributed in SWA/Namibia on ranches, game farms and conservation areas, and occur throughout the less settled parts of Botswana and Zimbabwe. In South Africa they still occur in the Kalahari Gemsbok National Park, the lowveld game areas and, occasionally, on the adjoining cattle ranches of the northern and eastern Transvaal; also in the larger game reserves of northern Natal where they have been introduced.

FEEDING BEHAVIOUR

Cheetahs depend on sight and speed for hunting, rather than on strength or stealth. They thus usually hunt only in daylight, early morning and evening being preferred, but they have also been recorded hunting on moonlit nights. They often watch for prey from a suitable look-out like an anthill and then approach cautiously until they are within range to make a sprint and catch. They are the fastest animals on land and can reach speeds of 110 km per hour over short stretches, but they lack stamina and are soon exhausted. It is essential for the success of their hunting technique that the prey should see them and stampede as it is easier to knock over a running animal — they do not normally attack any animal that stands its ground. They bowl their victims over by hooking a leg from under it using their sharp dew claws, or by pulling the animal over with a backwards and sideways pull that throws it off balance, again using the dew claws for gripping the prey. They kill by a suffocating grip on the throat, and their teeth seldom do more than break the skin of the prey; in the case of young animals they may suffocate them by holding their mouths over the muzzle of the victim. Their prey of choice are small to medium-sized, usually weighing less than 60 kg. They take impala, springbok, blesbok, steenbok, oribi, duiker, reedbuck, and also springhares, hares, guineafowl and ostriches. When several cheetah hunt together they take larger prey such as kudu cows, waterbuck, wildebeest and red hartebeest. After a chase they may rest for a while before starting to feed on the spot, or they may drag the kill under a shady bush before commencing to eat. They usually eat quickly, before any other predators can rob them of their kill, because they are virtually defenceless. They start feeding on the buttocks, shoulders or back and do not normally degut the carcass but tend to take what they require and leave the bones, head, skin and intestines. They can survive in extemely arid areas without water but drink regularly when it is available.

HABITS

Cheetah are more sociable than leopards but less so than lions. They may be seen alone, in pairs, or in small parties of up to six animals, occasionally as many as eight. The larger groups are usually a mother with cubs, or groups of cubs from the same litter which have become independent of their mother. Because they are vulnerable to other large predators, they are adept at hiding. They sleep at night and during the day under bushes or in clumps of long grass but do not use dens. When resting they usually lie on their sides, occasionally

---

Previous page: Cheetah have distinctive spots, as opposed to the rosettes of the leopard.

Opposite: This shows the colour variation known as the 'King Cheetah', in which the spots on the back have fused to form broad stripes.

raising a head to look around or sitting up from time to time to gaze around. They are fond of using anthills as observation posts, and they will even climb fallen or sloping trees for the same purpose. They are, however, not good tree climbers.

Cheetahs have a wide repertoire of communication calls, variously described as chirps, yaps or yelps, which are used in specific situations such as a mother calling her cubs, cubs calling their mother, or even a mother signalling her cubs to freeze or hide. In aggressive encounters they make a sharp yap or growl and they also purr loudly when contented or during play. The bonds between a mother and cubs and between siblings are particularly strong. Cubs becoming independent often move off as a group and remain together for some time. Cheetah females occupy a well-defined home range — possibly it is best described as a territory because they are aggressive towards other females, even their own adult daughters, and keep them out of their range. The females move around continually within the boundaries of their territory but they favour a central area. They mark their preferred vantage-points like anthills with urine and with their own dung. This spreads the owner's scent around for interpretation by other cheetah. Males are transient and move over much larger areas, but they do not appear to hold territories. Females are tolerant of wandering males and do not try and chase them away.

BREEDING

Cheetah females are extremely selective about mates — as has been learnt at great cost by many aspirant breeders of captive cheetahs. This may explain why males wander over great areas in order to come into contact with large numbers of females and so maximise the chances of meeting a female who will accept him as a mate. The oestrous condition of the female is betrayed by scent and by her behaviour towards the male. The cubs (2-5 in a litter) are born after a gestation period of 90–95 days. At birth the cubs are blind and helpless. They have an extremely well-developed, long, light-coloured mantle but are otherwise dark grey to sooty black in colour. They are hidden by the mother in patches of long grass or thick bush and do not accompany her until they are about six weeks old. As they are then still unable to hunt, they have to remain hidden while the mother hunts, and they hide in response to a particular low-pitched call by the mother; a different call will later induce the cubs to rejoin her. Cheetahs tend, in the Kruger Park, to produce cubs during the early dry season. This is perhaps to ensure that the nursing mother and the mother with a large litter of young cubs to feed enjoy the best hunting conditions. As the dry season advances, visibility improves and game concentrates near water, presumably making hunts more successful. This also ensures that the cubs are no longer at a helpless stage at the time of the late dry season grass fires, which may constitute a real threat to them. Cheetahs reach sexual maturity at about 15 months, and the cub may leave the mother at about 18 months.

ENEMIES AND DISEASE

Apart from man, the cheetah's main enemy is the lion; there are numerous records of lion killing cheetah adults and cubs, sometimes eating them, but mostly leaving the carcasses. Cheetahs are well aware of the lion's antipathy towards them and they will flee at the first sign of a lion and react nervously to lions' roaring. Cheetahs are also attacked on occasions by spotted hyaena, leopard and wild dog, and their cubs are particularly vulnerable. They may also be displaced from their kills by these carnivores and even also by brown hyaena. Apart from the usual range of parasites that most large carnivores seem to carry, cheetah are also susceptible to anthrax, tick fever and feline enteritis (cat flu).

Predators' Droppings in the Field

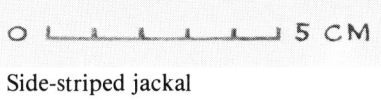

Side-striped jackal

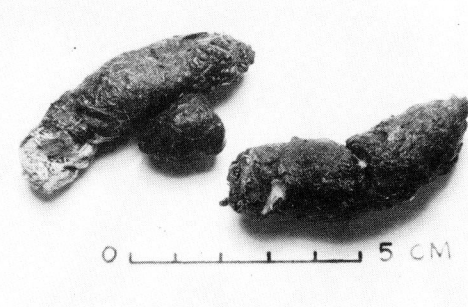

Black-backed jackal

Cape fox

Bat-eared fox

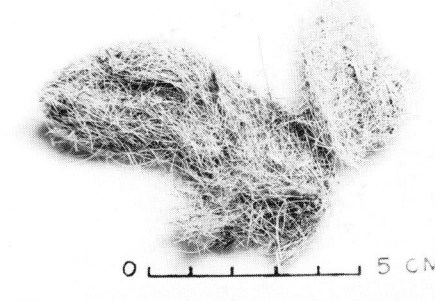

African wild dog

From top: Clawless otter, water mongoose, spotted-necked otter. Diam. of coin: 20 mm

Honey badger

Striped polecat

African civet

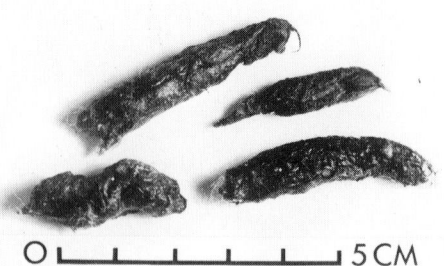

Small-spotted genet

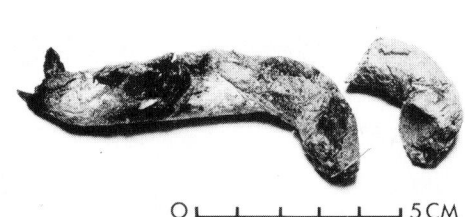

Rusty-spotted genet

White-tailed mongoose

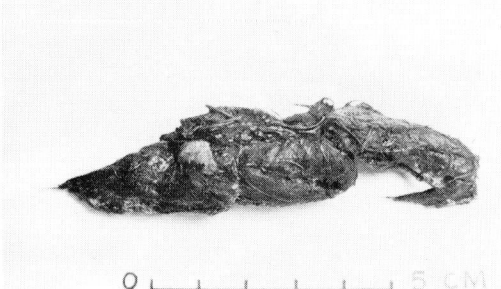

Meller's mongoose

Water mongoose

Large grey mongoose

Cape grey mongoose

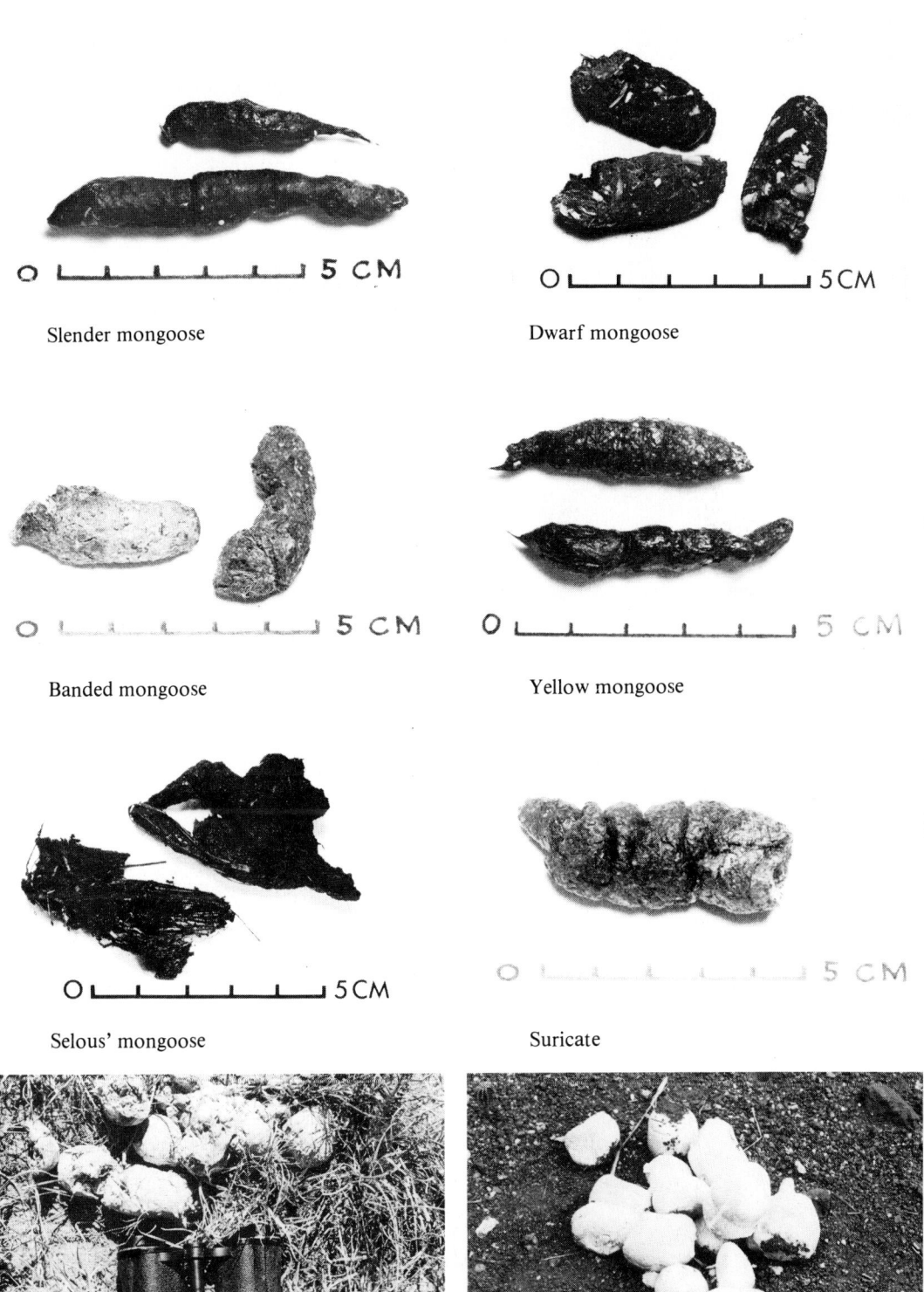

Slender mongoose

Dwarf mongoose

Banded mongoose

Yellow mongoose

Selous' mongoose

Suricate

Spotted hyaena

Brown hyaena

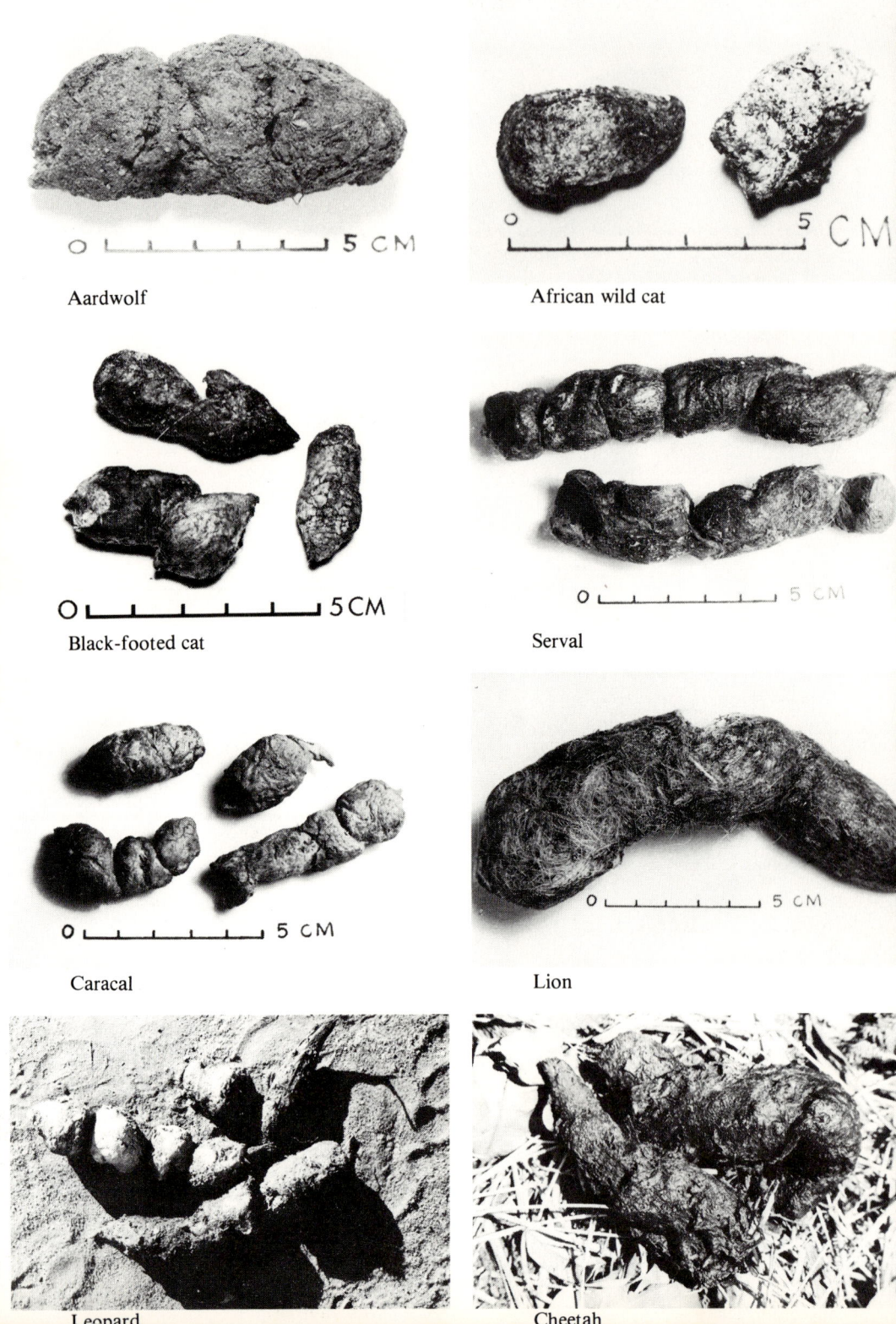

Aardwolf

African wild cat

Black-footed cat

Serval

Caracal

Lion

Leopard

Cheetah

LIST OF SCIENTIFIC NAMES OF ANIMALS
MENTIONED IN THE TEXT

African hawk-eagle	*Hieraaetus fasciatus*
Antbear	*Orycteropus afer*
Bateleur	*Terathopius ecaudatus*
Black eagle	*Aquila verreauxii*
Black rhinoceros	*Diceros bicornis*
Blesbok	*Damaliscus dorcas*
Blue wildebeest	*Connochaetes taurinus*
Buffalo	*Syncerus caffer*
Bullfrog	*Pyxicephalus adspersus*
Bushbuck	*Tragelaphus scriptus*
Bushpig	*Potamochoerus porcus*
Canerat	*Thryonomys* sp.
Cape cobra	*Naja nivea*
Cape eagle owl	*Bubo capensis*
Chacma baboon	*Papio ursinus*
Chanting goshawk, dark	*Melierax canorus*
Clawed toad	*Xenopus laevis*
Cobra	*Naja* sp.
Courser	*Rhinoptilus* sp.
Crocodile	*Crocodylus niloticus*
Crowned eagle	*Stephanoaetus coronatus*
Dassie, rock	*Procavia capensis* and/or
and/or yellow-spotted	*Heterophyrax brucei*
Dik-dik	*Madoqua* sp.
Duiker	*Sylvicapra grimmia*
Dune molerat	*Bathyergus suillus*
Eland	*Taurotragus oryx*
Elephant	*Loxodonta africana*
Elephant shrew	*Elephantulus* sp.
Francolin	*Francolinus* sp.
Fruit bats	*Epomophorus* sp. or
	Rousettus sp.
Fur seal	*Arctocephalus pusillus*
Gemsbok	*Oryx gazella*
Giant eagle owl	*Bubo lacteus*
Giraffe	*Giraffa camelopardalis*
Golden mole	*Amblysomus* sp.
Ground squirrel	*Xerus inauris*
Grysbok	*Raphicerus* sp.

Guineafowl *see* Helmeted guineafowl

Hare *see* Scrub hare and Red rock hare	
Hartebeest *see* Red hartebeest	
Harvester termites	
	Hodotermes mossambicus
Helmeted guineafowl	*Numida meleagris*
Hippopotamus	*Hippopotamus amphibius*
Honeyguide	*Indicator indicator*
Impala	*Aepyceros melampus*
Klipspringer	*Oreotragus oreotragus*
Korhaan	*Eupodotis* sp.
Kudu	*Tragelaphus strepsiceros*
Lechwe	*Kobus leche*
Leguaan	*Varanus* sp.
Mamba	*Dendroaspis polylepis*
Martial eagle	*Polemaetus bellicosus*
Mole *see* Golden mole and molerat	
Molerat	*Cryptomys* sp.
Mountain reedbuck	*Redunca fulvorufula*
Nyala	*Tragelaphus angasii*
Oribi	*Ourebia ourebi*
Ostrich	*Struthio camelus*
Pangolin	*Manis temminckii*
Porcupine	*Hystrix africaeaustralis*
Puku	*Kobus vardonii*
Python	*Python sebae*
Reedbuck	*Redunca arundinum*
Red hartebeest	*Alcelaphus buselaphus*
Red rock hare	*Pronolagus* sp.
Roan antelope	*Hippotragus equinus*
Sable	*Hippotragus niger*
Scrub hare	*Lepus saxatilis*
Sharpe's grysbok	*Raphicerus sharpei*
Shrew	*Crocidura* sp.
Springbok	*Antidorcas marsupialis*
Springhare	*Pedetes capensis*
Squirrel	*Paraxerus* sp.
Steenbok	*Raphicerus campestris*

Sun spider	*Solpuga* sp.	Warthog	*Phacochoerus aethiopicus*
		Waterbuck	*Kobus ellipsiprymnus*
Tawny eagle	*Aquila rapax*	White rhinoceros	*Ceratotherium simum*
Tsessebe	*Damaliscus lunatus*	Wildebeest *see* Blue wildebeest	
Vervet monkey	*Cercopithecus pygerythrus*	Yellowbilled hornbill	*Tockus flavirostris*
Vleirat	*Otomys* sp.		
Von der Decken's hornbill	*Tockus deckeni*	Zebra	*Equus burchellii*

INDEX

Aardwolf **94,** 96-7, *130*
*Acinonyx jubatus*120, **123, 124,** 125-6
Aonyx capensis **38,** 40-1
Atilax paludinosus **60,** 64-5

Badger, honey 36, **38, 39,** *127*
Bakoorjakkals 24
Bakoorvos 24
Bdeogale crassicauda 84
Boomsiwet 46

Canidae 15
Canis adustus 16, **17,** 19, *127*
    mesomelas **17,** 20-1, *127*
Caracal **106,** 109-10, **115,** *130*
Cat, black-footed 101-2, **104,** *130*
    small spotted 101
    wild, African 99-100, **103,** *130*
    wild, Cape 99
Cheetah 120, **123, 124,** 125-6, *130*
Civet, African 44-5, **48,** *128*
    palm 46, **49,** 51
    palm, two-spotted 46
    tree 46
Civettictis civetta 44-5, **48**
Crocuta crocuta 86-8, **92, 93**
Cynictis penicillata **71,** 77-8

Dog, hunting, Cape 26
    wild, African 26-30, **28,** *127*
Draaijakkals 22
Dwergmuishond 73

Felidae 98
Felis caracal **106,** 109-10, **115**
    lybica 99-100, **103**
    nigripes 101-2, **104**
    serval **105,** 107-8
Fox, bat-eared 24-5, **27,** *127*
    Cape **18,** 22-3, *127*
    silver 22

Galerella pulverulenta **61,** 67-8
    sanguinea 69-70, **72**
Genet, large-spotted 54
    rusty-spotted **50,** 54-5, *128*

small-spotted **50,** 52-3, *128*
Genetta genetta **50,** 52-3
    tigrina **50,** 54-5
Geelmeerkat 77
Grootkolmuskejaatkat 54
Groot grysmuishond 66
Groot witstertmuishond 56
Grysmuishond, Kaapse 67

Helogale parvula **62,** 73-4
Herpestes ichneumon **61,** 66
Hiëna, bruin 89
    gevlekte 86
Hunting dog, Cape 26
Hyaena, brown 89-90, **91,** 95, *129*
    spotted 86-8, **92, 93,** *129*
Hyaena brunnea 89-90, **91,** 95
Hyaenidae 85

Ichneumia albicauda 56-7, **59**
Ichneumon, Cape 66
Ictonyx striatus 32-3, **37,** *127*

Jackal, black-backed **17,** 20-1, *127*
    saddle-backed 20
    side-striped 16, **17,** 19, *127*
    silver-backed 20
Jakkals, Bakoor 24
    Draai- 22
    Maanhaar- 96
    Rooi- 20
    Silwer- 22
    Witwas- 16
Jagluiperd 120

Kleingrysmuishond 67
Kleinkolmuskejaatkat 52
Kleinwitstertmuishond 79
Kommetjiesgatmuishond 64

Leeu 111
Leopard 117-19, **122,** *130*
Lion 111-14, **116, 121,** *130*
Luiperd 117
Lutra maculicollis 42, **47**
Lycaon pictus 26-30, **28**

Lynx, African 109

Maanhaarjakkals 96
Meerkat 80
  geel- 77
  graatjie 80
  rooi- 77
  stokstert- 80
Mellivora capensis 36, **38,** 39
Miershooptier 101
Mongoose, banded **71,** 75-6, *129*
  bushy-tailed 84
  dwarf **62,** 73-4, *129*
  Egyptian 66
  grey, Cape **61,** 67-8, *128*
  grey, large **61,** 66, *128*
  marsh 64
  Meller's 58, **60,** 63, *128*
  red 77
  Selous' **72,** 79, *129*
  slender 69-70, **72,** *129*
  water **60,** 64-5, *129*
  white-tailed 56-7, **59,** *128*
  yellow **72,** 77-8, *129*
Muishond, borselstert- 84
  dikstert- 84
  dwerg- 73
  gebande 75
  groot grys- 66
  groot witstert- 56
  Kaapse grys- 67
  kleingrys- 67
  kleinwitstert- 79
  kommetjiesgat- 64
  Mellerse 58
  rooi- 69
  swartkwas- 69
  water- 64
  witstert- 56
Mungos mungo **71,** 75-6
Muskejaatkat, grootkol 54
  kleinkol- 52
  rooikol- 54
Mustelidae 31

Nandinia binotata 46, **49,** 51

Otocyon megalotis 24-5, **27**
Otter, clawless **38,** 40-1, *127*
  clawless, Cape 40
  spotted-necked 42, **47,** *127*

Otter, groot 40
  klein 42

Palm civet 46
Palmsiwet 46
Panthera leo 111-14, **116, 121**
  pardus 117-19, **122**
Paracynictis selousi **72,** 79
Poecilogale albinucha 34-5, **37**
Polecat, striped 32-3, **37,** *127*
Proteles cristatus **94,** 96-7

Ratel 36
Rhynchogale melleri 58, **60,** 63
Rooijakkals 20
Rooikat 109
Rooikolmuskejaatkat 54
Rooimuishond 69

Serval **105,** 107-8, *130*
Silwerjakkals 22
Silwervos 22
Siwet 44
Siwetkat 44
Skunk 32
Slangmuishond 34
Stinkmuishond 32
Strandjut 89
Strandwolf 89
Suricata suricatta 80, **81,** 83
Suricate 80, **81,** 83, *129*
Swartkwasmuishond 69
Swartpootkatjie 101

Tierboskat 107

Vaalboskat 99
Viverridae 43
Vulpes chama **18,** 22-3

Watermuishond 64
Weasel, African 34
  striped 34
  white-naped 34-5
Wild cat, *see* Cat, wild
Wild dog, African 26-30, **28,** *127*
Wildehond 26
Witkwasjakkals 16
Witstertmuishond 56

Zorilla 32